To Sally —

So sorry to hear
of your HEARTBREAK, but
you will move through it,
in time.

This is not a bereavement
book but it might contain
some ideas for you.

All the best,

8/02

The Good Bye Book

How To Heal A
Broken Heart
In 30 Days

By Howard Bronson and Mike Riley

The Listening Institute

National Market Makers, Inc., d.b.a.The Listening Institute
Book Website URL (address): *http://www.byebyelove.com*

Library of Congress Cataloging-in-Publication Data

Bronson, Howard F., 1953-
Riley, Michael D., 1941-
   The Good Bye Book: How To Heal A Broken Heart In 30 Days
   ISBN 0-9635378-2-2 (PBK)
   1. Self-help 2. Relationships 3. Break-up, separation, divorce
I. Title
Library of Congress Card Number: 00 - 190915

Book editing, layout and design by Mike Riley
Printed in the United States of America

Publications of The Listening Institute are available at quantity discounts for use in sales promotions, and for educational purposes. For more information, write to the Director of Sales at The Listening Institute, 1808 Pier Avenue, Santa Monica, CA 90405. Or contact your local book dealer.

Dedication

This book is dedicated to
our children.

The Good Bye Book

Table Of Contents

The Good Bye Book

INTRODUCTION

"Good bye." What a strange way to start a book. But that's where our usefulness to you will begin: when you say that very significant "good bye" which means "finally, it's over. This is the end of an us. I am not going to go back there again. I can't. Or I won't."

After that, a certain door closes for the very last time, or a telephone handset is placed back in its cold, hard cradle, leaving only stillness and that ache of a final good-bye. It's too soon to be tempered with any faint flecks of hope that it's now time, perhaps even past time to begin to move on.

For those who are lucky enough to become adolescents without suffering the loss of a parent or other close family member, the pain of the end of our first romantic love often introduces us to deep emotional pain. No matter how many more times we may face that same pain again, an emotionally healthy person knows that pain is the irresistible partner to our losses in love.

Now, judging by the fact that you're reading this book, you've come face to face with that same pain once again or perhaps for the very first time. So you've purchased this book to help you to tip the balance from desolation to hope, all in just thirty days. Don't expect a perfectly linear process; you won't necessarily feel better with each new day. There may be times when your recovery will hurt. If you've ever suffered from frostbite and then come into a much warmer place, the first thing you'll experience is pain before your normal feelings return.

Who This Book Is For

This book's method is intended for those who have suffered the end of a love relationship, and who want to make a more effective recovery. It doesn't matter whether it was you or the other person who decided to withdraw. It doesn't even matter if you've left your old lover for another. If you've shared a deep and special intimacy with someone, and now that intimacy has ended, you will suffer a loss equal to losing all of the meaning that relationship once had for you. And if you can't learn from your own mistakes which played a part in that loss, your mistakes will pursue you in hauntingly familiar ways.

Your loss may provoke a wide assortment of negative emotions. Your specific feelings will depend on the way you parted. Shame, grief, fear, loneliness, rage, jealousy, vengefulness, scorn, and humiliation, felt alone or in combination, are just some of the dark side emotions which may sit at your bedside. But so long as these emotions haven't gotten the best of you, so long as you know that your pain will pass in time, we can help you.

Three realizations will guide all of the people who may gain from this book out of their pain:

1) "My once-primary romantic relationship is now really over."

2) "The end of this relationship really is causing

me emotional pain."

3) "I want to make this pain come to a healthy and productive end as soon as I can."

Notice that healing first requires that you must accept that your intimate relationship is over.

Done. Ended. Finished.

If you believe you can end an important romantic relationship by immediately becoming "just friends," our first piece of advice is to forget this idea. When the romantic commitment which underlies a loving relationship dies, it almost always takes quite a while for the person who feels "dumped" to recover their balance.

Who This Book Is Not For

Since you must acknowledge that your relationship has ended to make use of this book, you must face the truth. This book is not for people who want to cheat on themselves. You can no longer afford to occasionally be intimate with your ex. You certainly can't continue to live together (the horror stories told by people who make this mistake really would curl your hair). Don't use money troubles as an excuse to continue to live together. Get out, now, while you still can. Put away that ring, the "cute couple" photo, and any lingering references to the two of you as a couple. That means no late night phone calls to each other just "'cause you're lonely." Or worse, making those "anonymous" calls where you just dial and then listen to hear your ex's voice say "Hello? Hello? Hello?" (Click)

The longer you put off facing the pain, the more

difficult that pain will be to deal with.

And if you catch yourself secretly stalking your ex to get another glimpse of the one you've "lost," get professional help soon. Stalking is a menacing form of potentially dangerous aggression. It is in no way an expression of love.

This book should not be the only remedy sought by people with deep and abiding emotional wounds. We include those people who are:

• Addicts, to sex, drugs or alcohol. Don't forget that denial is easy for an addict to hide behind. If in doubt, we urge you to ask a non-user friend or relative who knows you well if you have an addiction problem. And this time, try very hard to listen and if need be, to get the help and support you need so you can learn to give and receive love in a healthy way in the future.

• Abusers, or victims of abuse. If you have inflicted physical harm on a lover, or been so abused by another, you need additional help.

• People with depressive or bipolar conditions. Anyone who has had a long-standing history of periodic or chronic depression, that may reflect in a long history of relationship-sabotage.

• Anyone who feels irrational urges to harm themselves or another person, or who has urges which threaten to become uncontrollable.

At the very least, we urge any readers who fall into one or more of these classifications to seek help from a group of people with similar problems. Our award-winning Website at *http://www.byebyelove.com*

contains a page full of listings of national organizations that can put you in touch with others who share these challenges. It also can help you find experienced professionals who can help you to come to terms with your pain. For those who can afford it, personalized professional help is also worth considering, whether just from talking with your family doctor or in the form of brief or extended psychotherapy.

Why You Need To Call End Contact

If your relationship truly is over, you've got to give yourself a chance to recover as soon as you can. The person you've parted from is like a drug to you now. Another "hit" will only maintain your addiction. Accept that it's over, now.

For some, facing with the need to end contact with their ex will happen in painfully protracted stages. This is particularly true when a parting may lead to divorce. The full price of such endings may take a lifetime to pay. Misgivings and second thoughts are natural, and often wise. But when a final parting is clearly the only way for either party to actively pursue the prospect of happiness, a complete break is the best and often only way. Forget about scripting a perfect parting, there's no such thing. When it's time to end it, just do it, and move on.

Do you want to have a chance to develop a new relationship with your ex someday? That's possible. A significant percentage of all marriages that result in divorces conclude with remarriage to the same partner. But before that can happen on a stable and enduring basis, you've got to give both of you a chance to recover a fresh and independent perspective. Stay away while you heal. The only circumstances under which you should maintain contact after parting is for the sake of any children parented by the two of you, or to negotiate the division of mutual assets. If you have worked together, see if you can find new employment or get reassigned to an area where your exposure to each other will be kept to a minimum. Whatever you do, do not look for excuses to make any unnecessary contacts.

When will you heal? It will begin when you're able to pass more than an hour, ideally a full day, with no thoughts of your recent loss. And if your ex is really a decent person, you'll have fully recovered when you're able to forgive as well as forget.

This book can help you to do that on a timely basis. You'll be well on your way to this goal in no more than thirty days if you do what we suggest.

What This Book Promises

We do not claim that our method can relieve your pain on a fixed schedule. Grieving and growing happen differently for everyone, and for every relationship that ends. Of course it's not wise to attempt to suppress your feelings for the sake of meeting anyone's emotional timetable for your recovery.

However, most people in good emotional health who use our method can at least "see the light at the end of the tunnel" within roughly a month of ending even lifelong relationships. Perhaps you'll still continue to ride an emotional roller coaster after that time, but the dips and peaks should no longer have the power to make you sick to your stomach.

Even without our method, your status as "a poor

victim" will usually begin to lose its effect over your friends and family by the end of a month. Any ebbing of their expressions of sympathy will decrease any incentive you might otherwise have to cling to the ideas that you're a martyr or perpetual victim. For most people, even those who don't have the benefit of using our book, one month is often enough time for them to begin the natural progression through the customary stages of grieving and healing. Naturally, this may not be the case if an untimely death caused your loss, or if complex and heated dealings with divorce attorneys are necessary to protect your rights.

Exceptions aside, by using our book your recovery prospects will get even better. If you carefully employ our methods day by day, you can enhance your mental and physical health for the rest of your life. You can come out of your current suffering enriched with powerful new insights. You may even discover a remarkable new strength and resilience, thanks to the willpower that you will have exercised as never before.

Why Our Method Works

Others who write about recovering from relationship losses usually focus their counsel only on the emotional aspects of healing. Our focus will be broader. And we've tried very hard to make this book easy to read, and use, even by people who are distracted by powerful feelings of emotional pain. We promise that you won't find any maddening happy talk, "poor you" boo-hooing, or obscure psychobabble in these pages either.

What you will find is that the advice offered in this book is dramatically different. The text at its core of course teaches down to earth and practical ways to turn your negative emotions into fuel for an important spurt of personal growth.

But we don't stop there. Our advice to you differs most because it's holistic. We're going to give you a host of tools that will help repair your body as well as your spirit. These tools will help you to conquer your greatest enemies at this time. These enemies are stress and despair, which can lead to a slump into clinical depression.

Many of the drug-free methods we outline for beating stress and depression have been scientifically proven (yes, some even in rigorous double blind tests) as almost sure cures for the blues. Other methods we'll teach you have been proven down through the ages to be powerful ways to elevate your spirit. Some can carry you to the highest reaches that human consciousness can attain.

We don't want you to just settle for freedom from pain. We'd like to lead you to better ways to experience everything in your life.

How To Use This Book

To get the most from this book, you need to understand the way we put it together. Our counsel comes in two forms, offered by two authors, each in his own way.

Howard Bronson has authored a primer, a book in itself that provides a series of meditations and reflections on your process of grieving and growth. Day by day, Howard's counsel will guide your emotions through an evolutionary process that will help you to distill your pain into insight, and finally into forgiveness and wisdom.

Mike Riley has developed a series of "Tips" that prescribe self-enhancing behaviors dealing with everything from what you eat, to how you sleep, even down to how you breathe. The tip on making your own plan of action is one you should read right away. It will explain how to use the other tips in greater detail.

Basically, though, we can tell you right now that the best way to use this book is as they say in Alcoholics Anonymous: simply use it "one day at a time." Instead of having chapters, "The Good Bye Book" is organized into a series of thirty essays and tips, one for each day of a thirty-day period.

Organizing the book into a thirty-day period makes common sense in terms of the way we live our emotional lives. Each month of our days is a bit like a novel. You can also see it as a full cycle, led by the moon into a form that's a full circle, complete and whole in itself. You don't have to turn to the Zodiac or other New Age imagery to see the month as more than a metaphor. Just ask a woman about the power of her menstrual cycle. Or consider what that cycle implies about humans having an underlying biological mating cycle that lasts roughly thirty days.

By the same token, each day of our lives is like a story that begins and ends with some dreams. The two most important themes that unite all of these stories are that, first, we ourselves are ultimately responsible for all of the people who enter and leave all of our days. And second, that knowing when and how to take action is the key to resolving all of our conflicts. We're here to help you decide which actions will be most helpful in leading you out of trouble.

You can use the book in addition to your work with a psychotherapist or mutual support group. But most of our readers will use only this book and the counsel of friends as the foundation stones for their "do it yourself" recovery programs.

Why Turn To Us? Try: "Ask Your Dad"

One of the most common challenges we've encountered in the course of our preparation of this book goes something like this: "what qualifies you guys to give anybody advice on how to recover from the collapse of a romance?" It's an interesting challenge in several ways.

For one thing, most of the people who have asked us this question seem to assume that there are special qualifications required to offer others counsel on better solutions to life's emotional problems. We don't agree with this assumption. And in fact, most people act in ways that suggest that they don't, either.

Think about it this way: when you find you have an emotional problem, seeing a psychotherapist probably won't be the first thing you do. Before taking such an expensive step (which bears no guarantee of success, in any event), you are more likely to review your problem with people whose judgment you trust. And those trusted figures may even include a newspaper columnist or media personality like Ann Landers, Abigail VanBuren, "Dr. Ruth," "Dr. Joyce," "Dr. Laura," or even an Internet scribe like Lynn "Breakup Girl" Harris.

Which brings us to another interesting assumption behind the challenge to our authority in this field: we're guys. All of the popular figures who offer counsel to people dealing with the pain at the end of a relationship are women.

Why is that? Is it even wise? Isn't there room in the American marketplace of ideas about consolation and romance recovery for strong male voices to be heard as well as female ones? Is there likely to be any difference in content or outcome between genders in the quality of their counsel? We invite you to read this book and judge this question on your own.

Or ask your father what he thinks the answer might be.

If your family is like ours, other family members may have already suggested that you "ask your dad" about your problem. If he is like our late fathers were, his counsel would be peppered with pragmatism. Though loving, his perceptions are less likely to be overburdened with sympathy, giving his words a sense of balance and objectivity.

That's exactly the note we sought to strike here.

So if you ask us why we qualify to assist you, we'll tell you that we think we qualify at least as well as most of the leading lights who now offer "advice to the lovelorn" on a regular basis, for a variety of reasons:

• We each have survived long enough to have experienced any number of successful and failed romantic relationships in our own personal lives. Riley's nearly sixty. Bronson's just a decade younger. Thanks to "The Sexual Revolution" and its inevitable consequences, we've both had the opportunity to closely observe literally thousands of our friends' and associates' romantic relationships blossom and wither. We have both thought deeply about those experiences, and we both like to believe we're a little bit wiser as a result.

• We have both maintained our faith in the prospect of finding and maintaining love relationships which can enrobe our spirits in warmth and joy. Riley feels fortunate to have found such a person in Elizabeth, his mate of twenty years. Bronson is still seeking his answer. Riley respects the increasingly joyful, responsible, and creative way Bronson is now going about his quest for the last love of his life.

• Both of us failed at our first marriages. Our divorces were less unpleasant than hot acid baths. But far more instructive. We've learned enough to know the incredibly high emotional prices we paid for each of our own many mistakes.

• We're both fathers. We have kids of both sexes ranging in age between adolescence and young adulthood. We're proud of the fact that these people respect us enough to frequently ask our counsel when their own quests for love lead them into a romantic blind alley.

• We're both experienced journalists who have spent years reporting on developments in psychology and other social sciences. We currently write for an audience of doctors and other health care professionals, including psychotherapists and psychiatrists of every size and shape.

• Bronson is well known as an author on the subject of bereavement and recovery. His previous books on these topics include *Early Winter*, written on the occasion of the death of his father, and *Dog Gone*, which deals with the loss of a much beloved pet. Each of these books have counseled and consoled tens of thousands of readers.

• We're a couple of businessmen who have each run successful businesses of our own. This experience has taught each of us the importance of quickly finding practical answers to problems, and communicating those answers to people in a manner that encourages effective remedial actions.

• We have also been paid well by some of the biggest and most successful companies in the world to provide our counsel about commercial applications of advanced psychological research. Our clients have included Procter & Gamble, American Express, Westinghouse, Coca-Cola, Microsoft, and many other Fortune 500 firms.

• Both of us are recognized experts on creativity. Bronson is best known as the author of the bestselling books *Good Idea, Now What?* and *Great Idea, Now What?* Riley holds several U.S. patents in fields ranging from computer testing systems to filters and vacuum bags to audio amplifiers. As you use this book, we hope you will find our restless search for better ways to do things is evident in the solutions we've suggested. Like "Divorce Showers."

• Oh, yes, our academic backgrounds. Both Bronson and Riley earned undergraduate degrees with majors in Psychology. Our graduate degrees are in Journalism, Riley's from Northwestern, Bronson's from Boston College. Bronson has also done postgraduate work in Psychology, at the University of Denver. Neither of us has a graduate degree in Clinical Psychology, Social Work, or Medicine. But then, neither do most of the most popular dispensers of this kind of advice.

We actually have drawn more heavily from sources who might be classed as philosophers or physiologists, business people or mystics, than from what passes for wisdom in the world of psychotherapy. The influence of such sources is not just due to psychology's failure to qualify as a predictive science. We also happen to believe that even poets have useful insights into the human condition.

Validation And Valediction

But enough about us. We look forward to helping anyone who is willing to invest a modest amount of time and energy in acting on our counsel. As we mentioned, portions of our method have been tested by time, or on thousands of people in clinical trials. And for those we have counseled with our methodology, we have been told by all whom have used our counsel to any significant degree that they think they feel better as a consequence.

If you'd like to share details of your own experience with using our counsel, we'd appreciate hearing your comments. Send anything you care to share with us to the following Internet address: webmaster@byebyelove.com. And any time you might wish to get a refresher course or our latest tip on recovery, please visit our Website at

http://www.byebyelove.com

We'll be waiting there for you.

In the interim, you have our sincere best wishes for a speedy recovery of your ability to give of yourself freely and wisely, in love and in life.

Mike Riley and Howard Bronson

Day 1 Independence

The Emotional Circus

Your first reaction to the end of your relationship is likely to be shock. As soon as the shock wears off, grief arrives. Next, a whole emotional circus stirs: "I'm free. I'm relieved. Yet I'm devastated. I'm furious, hopeful, afraid." Your feelings may broaden into a multicolored panorama. They may include everything from the awesome sense of liberation you felt as a kid on the last day of school, to the nightmare sense that you've just failed your final exam. Back and forth...

That is, until someone thoughtlessly says something about "the work you have to do." That's when dread may set in. Your precious relationship has just died, and now someone else wants to sentence you to hard labor.

But please, relax. Hopefully you won't encounter such callousness on Day One of your recovery. For better and for worse, your liberation has arrived: it's your Independence Day. As soon as you can bear to share the news of your loss with friends and other loved ones, you 're more than likely to find sympathetic support — for at least today.

So prepare yourself. Soon enough, some self-appointed Calvinist will remind you of the work you have to do: "You have to work on yourself." Or more primitively: "You gotta do *the work*." Your reaction of dread will be deepened by the serious tones in which this grim advice is usually offered. At best, "*the work*" will sound like doing chores for Mom, as though you must take out all of your emotional garbage. Phew!

Skeptics might well deny the need: "The work? What work? I was in a romantic relationship for quite a while. For much of that time, it was good and reward-ing." And now, "the work" is supposed to help you become a whole person again, one who ultimately can be open to the prospect of a new and perhaps more enduring romance.

Is the impulse to deny this "work" stuff some-thing to feel guilty about? No. At the ultimate level of insight, you must always remember that you are whole and complete, a perfect person, destined to be just as you are.

Using the guidance of the authors of this book, your next 30 days will see you through a journey of self-recovery. You'll not be overloaded with new ideas about love and human nature. Instead, you'll be strengthened with no work at all. If you want to build your body's muscles, you go to the gym. You work out. Here we offer a cerebral spa for your wounded emo-tions. It's designed to help you realize your will's healing strength and ability to reintegrate the pieces of your broken heart.

Helpful Hurters

So what about this work stuff that others talk about? How long do you have to do it? Why bother? As some people speak about it, their ideas of "work" sounds like a prison sentence. All you did was lose or outgrow a love. Now you need to begin the new adventure of healing. Why should you have to do hard labor for this? The growing sense of confinement that such ideas of "work" may inspire could just add to your pain and confusion.

Everyone will seem eager to give you easy answers. Too few of those answers will make complete and immediate sense. Your sole certainty is that you hurt, really hurt, right now. That which was most comfortable has been wrested away from you. You find yourself in murky darkness. You need strong, clear light, yet all those near you have to offer are candles and matches.

And you're in a susceptible state. Sad songs make sense like never before. Whether you feel vindicated and defiant or defeated for all time, you may be more wide open than usual to new vulnerabilities. Your judges and advisors hurt because their judgments can imply that your broken spirit requires long winded, obscure instructions about how to get through these dispiriting times.

If you ask for it, many layers of freely available advice will arrive from all sides: face-to-face, e-mail, voice mail, or ordinary mail, even as rumors passed on the wind. There's so much of this kind of advice out there, if you listen to all of it your confusion will certainly deepen. You may find so much advice buzzing this way and that way that it makes you to forget one simple fact. That's the trustworthy words of the good witch of Oz, which offer all of the wisdom you'll ever need: "You had the power within you all along."

Your confusion with the advice you're being offered may well be well founded. Your advisors' motives may range from true generosity to barely concealed power plays. At best, people see offering advice to the afflicted as doing their own good work, especially when it's easy to offer. And offering love advice to others who suffer makes us feel better about ourselves. Offering advice also can be a token in a contest for power, with the advisor really saying "I'm better than you, because I'm not suffering as you are. And I know how to get out of the trouble you're in. It's about time you followed my lead."

People who say "I'm sorry but I don't know what to tell you" might sound as though they really don't care. But they may be the most honest of all. Most of us want to help end the suffering of others, especially when it can be carried out in a mindless manner. "You'll be alright." "Men are like buses, there's a new one along every five minutes." "You weren't right for each other." "There's plenty more fish in the sea." Etcetera, etcetera, etcetera. All of which may make you think to yourself: "yeah, but how many of those fish are sharks in disguise?"

Truth and Proof

The truth is no one knows what's best for you. And there's a very good reason for that. No one really understands your personal experience like you do.

Also, many of us have been taught to think that intimately loving someone is a very complicated project. Such thinking can idealize the prospect of an enduring romantic relationship into an unattainable task. It can seem so difficult that some people may forego love altogether, while others blindly and hopelessly leap into new relationships without pause for reflection. Or they may feel their pain so profoundly that they fall into an extended depression. Down so far that all advice sails right over their heads.

The information age has both its rewards and consequences. Every book, tape or therapeutic seminar aspires to add to our knowledge base. The abundance of new data has potential benefits but our progress can collapse from the immensity of its weight.

The purpose of this guide is to lighten that load. The words and exercises you will find here are designed to take the weight out of the work in the breakup process. What little "work" we suggest is modest, and can help you to realize a wholeness you've never experienced before.

Some of your current advisors may view a breakup as being a kind of death. The erudite ones may even be able to break your breakup down into grid-like patterns, telling you of the phases you must go through to achieve peace and relational happiness once again.

Shock, Anger, Denial, Bargaining, and Resolution are the classic phases of grieving that attend a mortal loss. But what if you don't experience all of these feelings? Does that mean you haven't come to terms with the passage of a lover into your past? Of course not.

A breakup is not a death, except perhaps the death of one phase of your life, or of an illusion about love. And if you could correct that illusion in a short time, why should you then choose to stretch out the process?

Time presents a problem. The pursuit of emotional healing for its own sake has become so popular in the past few decades that many people spend far more time working at healing (or clinging to wounds) than at living and loving. The results are not always productive. Look for the downside in the next angry stranger you meet who tries to blame you, people like you, or even people like their parents or themselves, for all of his or her miseries. You'll also hear this pursuit reflected in the counsel that your recovery is likely to involve a long, drawn-out and often expensive process.

Or at least it was historically, as psychotherapists, psychologists, psychoanalysts and psychiatrists played the private pay game. Then suddenly, brief therapy happened, as managed care dictated a limited number of therapeutic visits. It seemed as though some therapists suddenly discovered they could get you back in the game after just three to five visits, versus the year or two or three that it used to require. Psychiatrists got even better, finding that one prescription could do the job for all time.

That's good. Better yet, for most people, psychotherapy for romantic recovery involves an even faster process. After exactly no visits at all, they're on their way to a happier, healthier life. Those are our kind of people. Strong, confident, well-balanced and self-reliant people. Or folks who are determined to become so, despite their pains.

The unhappy end of an intimate relationship can generate some of the ugliest ironies you will ever experience. Get ready. The person you loved, held and cared for, and were most intimate with, is now nothing but a fragile set of memories that will vanish into the mists of the future. What was so close is now moving away. One who was your best friend, must now act like a stranger, or even an adversary. How can this be? Why does this have to be? And how long must you waste time with such perplexing questions before you're willing to take some truly effective action for your current and future well being?

Get ready for the good part: your relationship's end gives you an opportunity to create the best time of your life; to learn but not linger, to heal but not hate.

In truth, you can't mourn the loss of someone who's still living. That's the bizarre paradox. Yet, traditionally we've often been advised to do exactly that. Why then should we be astonished to find that the process of pursuing such an unreal goal is never complete?

Hurt may linger long enough to color and contaminate all of your ongoing efforts to relate to other people. Watch out; your motives may be based on the desire to return to the comfort of the familiar. To the same easy, habitual ways that defined us, identified us, completed us. Or so we thought.

The need to restore the familiar may create the expectation that a new relationship will be better just because it's new. We'll just make a few adjustments and everything will be just fine. But what happens when the new experiences just don't click and we can't achieve the comfort that we seem to remember we once had?

For most, perhaps you, that can mean running into the same dilemma all over again. Are you prepared to once again give up a piece of your heart? Keep it up, and ultimately you'll have nothing left to offer a new prospect but guarded mistrust. In essence, that new prospective lover will remain forever on trial for the many mistakes you made with your previous lovers.

Once you have made a genuine recovery, your new life and any new relationships you may undertake will be so much better not because they are new but because you've renewed your moorings. And because you have found the wiser and simplest path of remembering that because you're human, you already know how to love.

Can you become a virgin again? Perhaps not. But your ability to open yourself to a loving innocence can be recovered. Time, healing actions and the right kind of insights will make all the difference.

So on this first day, whether you're relieved or dejected, there is loss to be reckoned with. We urge you: don't do "the work," at least the work that everyone's screaming at you to do. You don't have the time, and it will only make you feel less capable than you really are.

Say good-bye to that work-myth just like you're saying good-bye to your ex and instead, let the insights and tips in this book help you to cut through the advice jungle. Let us help you uncomplicate the process. Our method will help you embrace a new vision and freedom over the next 30 days. A freedom to love and be loved in the ways you always wanted.

You've opened to day one, meaning that you're ready to make your heart whole again and move forward in your love life. So we're ready if you are. We begin by urging you to make the following pledge to nobody but yourself:

The Contract

I,_____, declare that I am sick of feeling that my heart is less than whole. I am going to stop feeling reduced, diminished, less than whole. I intend to feel myself grow once again. I do not want a mess of broken-heart pieces running my life for any reason. I want to love and be loved, on an enduring, fulfilling, and equitable basis. And perhaps even passionately, if my heart someday proves ready to take that chance once again.

For the next thirty days, I am going to do all the work required to repair my heart so I can move forward in my life. I am going to put the pieces back together better than I have ever done so before. I am going to become my own person: autonomous and whole.

I have no idea if my ex and I may someday get back together. It doesn't matter. I am going through with this breakup because I must end my old, self-destructive way of dealing with our relationship. I am not going to call or speak to my ex for any reason but to negotiate any unresolved terms of our parting, such as the custody of children or property. I know that any hopes for reconciliation that I may now entertain will cause me more hurt than will ending things *now*.

Over these next 30 days, I will reaffirm that I am fully worthy of being loved, that I deserve to be happy, and that no one is going to stop me from exercising these rights. I will rediscover the good and lovable things about myself and I will celebrate them. And I will gradually open myself to giving my love to others again, and be astonished to realize that even without romance, love always feels like something brand new.

Signed, (your name)

Now, for the rest of this day, think about this: You did what you could to be open for love. You were willing to risk exposing your heart. Celebrate that fact. By being willing to risk your safety for love, you showed yourself to be a creature of courage. Now you will be able to use that same courage to effect your recovery. And to love like a warrior again, if you wish, as you move to conquer your future.

Private Thoughts

Before you go to bed, make a list of private, even solitary indulgences that can or will make you happy. Be honest, if love is among them.

Contrast those things to how sad it is for love to end. Sure it hurts. But how joyous to know that all kinds of love are available for all of us who are ready to receive it!

It's not a crisis to experience sadness but merely another turn in the wheel of your life Sadness shows that you've risked your safety for joy. It's the risk of reaching out, of self-exposure, that gets us there when nature says it's time once again. It's a vitally poignant part of the ongoing story that composes a full and happy life.

Your life: pain, sorrow, regret, reflection, growth, triumph, peace. And around again.

For now, sadness and pain give proof that you're alive. Use them as tools to goad you to grow.

 . . . Make A Plan For Action

One of the best ways to prevent your sadness from slumping into depression is to take action. What action? That's up to you. Our job is to make suggestions, you make the choices. One of our first suggestions to you is to make a plan for your own rescue.

It's easy to do. Once done, your plan serves as a commitment you make to yourself. It says that "this is what I will do, and do again, and do as many times as I must, to make sure that I recover a balance of positive feelings about myself and about others, within a reasonable period of time." Don't worry if you can't do every thing you had planned at the outset, every day of the next month. Do the best that you can, and you'll begin to feel better within days.

Plan Your Attack

We suggest that you prepare to lay out your plan by skimming through all of the "Tips" which conclude each of the chapters of this book. Once you're done, make a list of all of those measures we've suggested that you plan to do regularly. That list is your action plan. Keep a copy of your plan by your bedside, and keep another copy where you work, where you can't avoid seeing it once or twice a day.

Then read the book again more carefully, but

only one successive chapter a day, for each day of the thirty days of your recovery. As you progress through the book, do those things on your action plan every day, or as often as you've promised you will. Your sense of confidence that your life and your emotions are manageable will increase in direct proportion to your ability to work out and stay with a program that suits your own needs.

The Basics

Of all of the steps we've advocated, here are the ones we think everyone should include in their own action plan as a necessary minimum:

1. Diet changes see page 69

2. Adequate sleep see page 44

3. Relaxation and meditation see page 137

4. Exercise see page 51

5. Proper breathing see page 120

6. Scaling see page 188

7. Anger management see page 95

8. Paradox see page 144

9. Time Plan see page 39

10. Humor see page 109

Elective Elements

Ultimately, the components of your action plan will be whatever items you select. Your list can of course include items that we haven't suggested but that you think might be useful. For example, why not plan to correct a habit that won't serve you well in these difficult times. It needn't be something major like smoking. For example:

• Stand up straight (always a good idea, one that will help you to breathe better, and subtly let others know you've got a sense of pride, dignity, and the self-discipline necessary to attend to your posture).

• Clean up your office and living space, to make yourself feel less like you're surrounded by confusion that's beyond your control.

• Get an air cleaner, to make your breathing exercises more appetizing.

What should go into your action plan? Any steps that you can do right now, or soon, that will make you feel better on a short-term basis. It's all up to you.

Day 2 Expression

The Mourning After

Waking up on the day after a break-up can be a rather grim affair. Most people emerge from the hiding place of their slumbers to the unhappy recollection that a large part of their life is now gone. It's the first day of "the mourning after" a loss.

Take that first moment of mourning to reflect on a fundamental truth: anyone who doesn't have the good sense to recognize what you have to offer doesn't deserve your time. Anyone who missed that point hasn't fully enjoyed the offering of your love.

This hurts. The pain of that hurt can virtually paralyze your will. But hard as it might seem to understand at this moment, your pain is not like dying at all. It's a sign that you are in fact, being reborn, healing from a very deep wound. With the right will, you are destined to grow stronger and more vital than ever before.

And if you're willing to be patient and active as you heal over time, you'll eventually discover that depression and inertia are bad choices people make to avoid their core issues. These choices express weakness, fear and anger instead of actively expressing healing, love, and hope.

Focus your energies on giving yourself credit for every step of your healing. Of course, at the beginning of your path out of pain, there's anguish. Your former lover's name and essence may constantly intrude into your consciousness. Over time, the name will fade as the wisdom of the lessons you've learned takes over. That's when joy and laughter will be your payback, the interest you've earned on your investment in thoughtful reflections on your feelings of intense sadness.

Whatever you choose for your life, a deeper understanding of what you're now going through will give you more self-reliance, strength and genuine joy in the future. A breakup can teach us so much about our goodness and value if we'll only take the time to think about the meaning and purpose for pain.

On the other hand, you may be feeling okay for the moment. You may even feel a sense of liberation. But most people also feel a sense of loss and a fear of loneliness. And they can certainly feel like they're mourning the death of a loved one. No matter what you feel, once again, remember that you're involved in a self-renewal that's disguised as grieving. But to achieve renewal, you must understand how it differs from the grieving process.

There is a hurt that cannot be denied but it does not follow the general course of grief. In breakups, we often jump from shock to anger and then linger in confusion for ages. Mix in a little denial and, well, we don't want to know about it. It's like a scary movie. We're there but we don't want to look at the ugly parts.

If you try to pretend that the pain just doesn't exist, you get yourself into the same jam all over again

– similar love, similar dynamics and similar heartache at the end.

It doesn't have to be that way but the problem is that you don't want to look at your pain any more than you have to. It's easier to see yourself as an innocent victim ("If only my ex wasn't so inflexible," etc.). You don't want the additional burden of having to feel responsible for mistakes you may have made, or sins you feel you've committed. That kind of honesty just hurts too much when you're in this vulnerable state.

But if you don't make an effort to understand what you're feeling, your own core truth, the pain is just going to linger. And why not face it now? Do it now, over the course of the next twenty-nine days, in an intelligent and self-supportive fashion. Our contention is that if you're simply willing to come to terms with your own true self within this time-frame, you won't have to remain trapped in the dark stages for very long.

Mourning can too easily devolve from being a healthy transitional passage into an inescapable trap that prevents relational progress. Through this guide, we're going to help you get free of this trap. But we have many days to evolve out of these darker feelings. The only goal for today is to have you take a glimpse of the things you're feeling at the moment, and to allow those feelings to happen, no matter what they may be.

If you feel the need to laugh, scream, cry or even curl up in a ball, do so. This is a day of gentle observation, and self-expression. Whatever you do, don't bottle up all your true feelings. Just let them come out and observe them, as if you were observing someone else.

The only rule is: THIS IS NOT A BLAME EXER-
CISE. Most especially, don't waste any time blaming
yourself. Breakups happen no matter who we are, or
what we do. And if you're willing to stop for a moment,
take a deep breath, and look at the signals you got over
time, and accept the possibility that it really was time to
say good-bye, you can begin to heal. Honesty carries
gusts of great opportunity beckoning from our future.
Feel these winds, breathe them in deeply, deal with the
truth and move on.

Notice too that emotions are often disclosed by a
very specific physical feeling, which accompanies them.
For example, a feeling of longing can be given away by
our gut, while a feeling of abandonment or broken-
heartedness can actually feel like a hole in our upper
chest. An emotion of self-blame or fear can feel like
paralysis.

In reviewing the past, remember that relationships are often like mirrors; our mates often reflect back
both our attributes and our faults. The following exercise will help you reflect back your own feelings in a
non-threatening fashion.

Pause For Reflection

Where are you?

Stop for a moment. Take a relaxing 'cleansing'
breath. Now, find a mirror and look at yourself. Deeply
look into your own eyes. What are you feeling right at
this moment? Does your face reflect those feelings?
What else does your expression show you about you?
What emotions can you read down deep in your eyes?

What do you feel in your gut? What do you feel

in your heart?

Remember these feelings. But don't stay mired in them. Be open to sometimes painful but much needed changes. Changing can feel like a wound because in fact, it exposes the most vulnerable parts of your being.

Look at those feelings, see them, and get to know them. But don't cling to them. Don't obsess. Just see them as clearly as you can, as a small rip in your fabric that merely needs to be gently repaired. You've had love and supportive compassion for another person, now it's time to turn that love inward in order to make your own personal repairs.

Now ask yourself, if there was a workable and grounded system for doing so, would you be willing to break free of your imprisoning negative feelings once and for all? Of course you would. But the problem with being human is that we're often afraid to look at our own shortcomings, and so things that otherwise could be resolved in no time remain trapped inside. Isn't it time to break that pattern?

Out With The Bad

It's time to purge yourself of all of your toxic feelings. You don't need them anymore. One very healthy way is to have a good cry. Here's how to use your weeping constructively, instead of letting it use you:

TIP ... Cry Till You're Dry

Feel like crying? Go ahead. It's *GOOD* for you.

It's not just good for an emotional release. As

strange as it may seem, the tears that are prompted by your heart-felt feelings of loss actually cleanse your system of toxins and waste. It's the same as eliminating solid and liquid wastes to purge toxins from the blood and intestines. A professor at the Colorado Medical School who has measured the chemical benefits of crying noted that many of those who "have a good cry" even look better soon afterward.

There's a chemical difference between the kind of tears our eyes produce for moisture or to remove a cinder, and the kind that we produce by crying. Crying tears are 30 times richer in manganese than blood is, for example. Biochemists say that manganese is only one of three such chemicals that are stored up by stress and flushed out by a good cry.

So it's no surprise that researchers have found that people who cry often are healthier. A 1980 study by Margaret T. Crepeau, ("A Comparison of the Behavior Patterns and Meanings of Weeping Among Adult Men and Women Across Three Health Conditions") at the University of Pittsburgh School of Nursing found that healthy people of both sexes are more frequent criers.

Frequent weepers also feel better about crying than do people with ulcers and colitis. Because depression often precedes a common cold, researcher Merl Jackel suspects that colds may be "symbolically repressed tears." Others have speculated that even asthma and hives may be linked with the suppression of tears.

As for emotional health and grief recovery, it's clear that tears help. For example, widows with associates who encouraged them to weep and express their heartfelt feeling recovered faster than those who lacked these expressive resources. Some researchers have speculated that widowed men die sooner after the death of a spouse than do widows because women are socialized to cry more freely (Helsing, Szklo, and Comstock, "Factors Associated with Morality after Widowhood," American Journal of Public Health, August 1981).

Others find that men die sooner than women do after any major stressful experience, such as a death in the family. Males' customary repression of feelings is commonly thought to account for such differences (W. Dewi Rees, "Bereavement and Illness," Journal of Thanatology Summer-Fall 1972).

"So what if crying is good for me," you may say. "I'm not a good crier." To which we reply that great criers are not born, they're made. Practice makes perfect. Here's an easy method that can quickly turn you into a real crier, expert class:

To do a proper job of flushing your feelings of loss, set aside fifteen private minutes a day to take care of your crying needs. To deliberately induce weeping, employ a method that's successfully been used to relieve the feelings of loss suffered by many elderly people in nursing homes:

1. Play some music that makes you feel sorrowful. Whether it's Prokofieff's Romeo and Juliet or the soundtrack from Titanic, listen to the most emotionally moving passage and feel just how sadly the music speaks to your spirit.

2. Place your right hand lightly on the upper center of your chest, close your eyes, and breathe in

small, short gasps. Do it just as though you are in the early phases of sobbing. You don't need to hyperventilate, just induce the feeling that you are now ready to cry.

3. As you breathe this way, think of something that makes you very sad. You don't need to think of your lost love. The contents of your thoughts don't matter as much as the results they produce: just so long as they make you sad enough to cry.

Some people, most often men who haven't cried in years, can hardly seem to stop crying once they start. Their extended weeping sessions may even last for several weeks, but each session for rarely more than twenty minutes a day. Don't panic if this should happen to you; it's okay. You just need to lower the pressure in your dammed up emotional reservoir to a safer level.

In fact, if you're like most people, you'll ultimately grow bored with crying about a fantasy drama starring your lost love. Oddly enough, that day will come more quickly if you force yourself to cry about him or her every day. The harder you try, the harder the story will get to cry about.

It's a fortunate fact that spilled milk spoils quickly. Sure, feel your feelings. Stay open to the natural evolution of your emotions. And realize that mourning sickness does not naturally produce a lifelong affliction. You really don't need to get trapped in mourning. Every moment you choose to spend grieving is a moment lost from the prospect of joyfulness.

Day 3 Indulgence

A "Poor Me" Holiday

Friends are going to hear a lot from you during this difficult period. And because they're your friends, they're still around. That's why they're willing to hear you talk on and on about yourself and your ex. Much of what you say is cleansing and these expressions of your feelings will help you make it through. But some of this litany is just ranting about an experience that you should both learn from and outgrow. If you keep rehearsing and perfecting your negative feelings, they'll never fade.

Look at it from a different perspective. If you have a sore throat that vitamin C & Echinacea could cure in four days, would you let it linger for weeks or months in which it could cause real harm? Likewise, if you could use a series of logical and proven steps to genuinely curtail your hurt feelings in a far shorter time frame, why on earth would you allow them to linger? Life really is too short for that.

So we've created a special holiday just for you. And that holiday is today. Call today your "Poor Me Day." Instead of feeling just a little bad for an extended period, why not have just one special day you use to indulge yourself for all of your suffering, in preparation for being done with it.

And why *should* you take a lifetime to lament love's cruel fate? It's like that 'work' thing again. And the more people like therapists who want to work on us, the more danger we have of becoming weakened. "Ya mean I'm such a mess that I have to work for a year at getting repaired?" That's not a very reinforcing message for your subconscious. So don't knock the Poor Me holiday idea until you've tried it.

Our schedule calls for only one "Poor Me Day" but you may have to do it again if you don't get it right the first time.

Remember those private indulgences you wrote down for Day One? How many of them can you do today? Can you just take a day off and do whatever you feel like doing? If you can, do so.

The goals of your free day will be twofold: your first goal will be to celebrate yourself, by being totally self-indulgent but *not* self-destructive.

The second goal of your free day will be to treat yourself like a vulnerable kid. Indulge all of your harmless impulses, all of your feelings.

Give yourself a day of rest and reflection. Laugh if you want, cry if you want. Settle in with a mental laxative, like watching soap operas or wrestling. Or even the Three Stooges. Eat lots of fiber, relax every muscle in your face. In short, release from within. Forget "work." Use your holiday for an intensive emotional detoxification.

You've been working hard to love one or more others. You're exhausted. So take a break. This is your holiday. Celebrate lovable you.

Don't waste your day lamenting might-have-beens or should-haves. Don't live in the fantasy of the past, no matter how good you can now make it seem in the theater of your mind. Odds are it was never as good as you'd like to think it was. So just let it all go and take a holiday from "Poor Me."

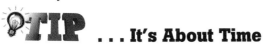 **. . . It's About Time**

You've probably already noticed that your feeling of grief ebbs and flows. The pain from your deep sense of loss can be triggered by internal and external events that you'll have little ability to manage. But if you can learn to predict when you're likely to hurt the most, you may have some success in preparing yourself to keep your pain from getting the upper hand.

You first need to recognize that there are times — times of the day, days of the week, months and seasons of the year — when you are more vulnerable to pain than you are at other times. Once you can predict the timing of your own emotional clock and calendar, you'll be better able to protect your own vulnerability.

Taking Inventory

The first step in setting up your own timely self defense plan is to take an inventory of your bad times.

What days of the week are hardest for you? Probably weekends, when no-one's around and the sound of silence can make you feel oppressively lonely. Or is it some other day that was special to you and your ex? Say, Fridays, when you'd meet after work?

Once you've identified your worst days, you

should immediately find an alternative activity that can fill up those empty hours with something that's equally fulfilling. Do you have anything that you've meant to do for a long time that you just haven't gotten around to — like taking a course, becoming a volunteer, or writing the Great American Novel?

Congratulations: you now have the free time. So get busy.

By the same token, what's the worst hour of the day for you? When you first wake up in the morning and realize you're still alone? So get a pet. Is it when you come home at night and no-one is there to greet you? So turn on some music you love as soon as you walk in the door. Is it after work when you still go to the spot where you always met your ex? Now that they're not there to join you, do you just leave alone and lonely? So don't even bother to stop there, until you can come and go without wanting to run into your ex and pick things up from where you went wrong.

Calendar Problems

Get ready for the period between Thanksgiving and New Year's. And don't forget Valentine's Day or early January's post-holiday slump. These are notoriously tough times to find yourself feeling alone or abandoned. If that's the time when you first find yourself alone, we hope you can find solace among loving family and friends who can help fill the void in your life with the tender affection you need at this time.

If you don't have such resources close at hand, try offering loving comfort to others whose needs may be greater than your own: volunteer your time to work serving free holiday meals at a local nursing home or at an organization that cares for the homeless or other unfortunates. Or volunteer at an animal shelter. Far from causing you more pain, such an experience could very well remind you of how truly fortunate you are, despite your truly temporary sense of profound loss.

Hard times are also often seasonally related. If you live in an area with bitter cold winters, or in an area with seasons that make for gray skies day after day, you could experience "seasonal affective disorder," or SAD — an extended depression that's triggered by too little sunlight. Some find relief by taking a vacation to a warm, sunny climate. Others make do with artificial lights that simulate sunlight. Some success has even been reported from use of a light under your bedcovers at night, shining up on the backsides of your knees.

No, we didn't make this up. If you're curious, ask your doctor what you should do if you think you feel blue because you're "under the weather," or perhaps just stuck in the wrong season.

Rediscovering Self-Respect

Did you work too hard to maintain your recent relationship? Bend over backward, swallow your pride, play the doormat to prevent any conflicts? Did you deny yourself or put down your power to please another? Or perhaps you were a rescuer: always ready to save your lovers from themselves, no matter how great the price you had to pay for them? Ever hopeful that you could change them for the better? That's too bad; few lovers who need rescuing respond as you'd hope. And let's be honest. Rescue acts are often control games in disguise. In the best kinds of love, you can just love and accept a lover, without having to manage their emotional baggage as well as your own.

When it feels like all that you are is not enough for the other person, you're not being appreciated for your own unique goodness. If the relationship is just too much work, face it. Your dearly beloved may just not be worthy of your precious time (at least as far as *you* are concerned).

Everyone has something that's essential to their own inner glory. But in an unhealthy or stale relationship, you can lose, sacrifice, or hide your inner lights because you're too busy dragging your mate out of the dark.

This is the day to relearn your value. It's a day for discovering all of the things you've learned over the past year or so, but have failed to give yourself credit for. This exercise will help you to further celebrate your personal value. We all have to stand at ease within ourselves before we can stand to love another.

How should you do this? Do something you really want to do, but have put off for too long. Clean out the garage, join a Salsa dance group, reconnect with friends you've neglected, or start building a house. It really doesn't matter what you choose to do, as long as it's something that's genuinely a part of you, something that you want to explore or create, something that you initiate all on your own.

Our sense of our own value is determined by who we are, and what we do. When we're in an unhealthy relationship, we often lose sight of who we are and as our identity becomes weakened, so does our ability to achieve those things that are central to us. It's easy to let go of our gifts when we're totally preoccupied with just staying afloat.

So get busy! Not merely busy-work-busy but productively busy. Do something that doesn't just occupy your time but find something that genuinely expresses and enriches the best that's within you. By doing this, you'll begin to become reacquainted with your personal uniqueness, with those lovable things that made you perfect in the first place.

Some suggestions:

1) It's best to invest your time in something that only you can complete on your own.

2) Make it something whose positive results will be around for a long time.

3) If you're able, make it something that creates new opportunities for you in the future.

No easy answers come to mind? Spend more time thinking. Yet for many, the project ideas will come very readily. Make a list of them all. When your list feels complete, choose the one thing you'll start first. When you know you have both the will and the means to complete your project, then begin it. Imagine that your project is like a train that will stop at only the right stations and pick up only the right passengers who can help you to get where you've elected to go.

And along the way, be your own best supporter. Make sure you do some kind little thing for yourself each day.

 . . . Get A Good Night's Sleep

Separations can have a couple of unexpected outcomes. As your body senses an emergency your mind might otherwise refuse to acknowledge, don't be surprised if you:

• Start losing weight at the rate of up to two pounds a week, and

• Start losing sleep, at the rate of up to four hours per night.

If these things happen to you, your response may be positive or negative to either or both. For example, losing a lover is a painful way to go on a diet, but if you needed to lose weight, it may be a welcome side effect. The experience is usually less harmful than using cigarette smoking for weight control, anyway.

The same kind of logic might arise if you find yourself able to sleep only half the night. Think of all the extra work you can get done, or the books you'll have the time to read, or those new movie rentals you've meant to catch up on.

But don't take that kind of thought too seriously. Self-induced fatigue can be deadly, if it prevails too long. It can impair your judgment, your driving skills, your impulse control, shorten your patience in the face of such stresses as difficult divorce negotiations, and lead to untypical outbursts of temper that can result in consequences that may damage you for years to come. Loss of sleep will also deprive you of the time you need for dreaming. Some scientists believe that the exercise that dreaming gives our brains helps to purge them of "residue," or problems, encountered the previous day.

Dr. William Dement, a Stanford University professor known as one of the world's leading authorities on sleep. Dement says that "There is plenty of compelling evidence supporting the argument that sleep is the most important predictor of how long you will live, perhaps more important than whether you smoke, exercise, or have high blood pressure or cholesterol level."

In short, to stay mentally and physically fit, you need to get a good rest every night of the week. For most, that means seven and a half to eight uninterrupted hours of sleep. Especially if you might otherwise be tempted to hang around some place where you can ease your loneliness by having a beer or three with people you really don't care about.

How do you accomplish that, when your body's alarms are ringing "stay awake" all night long? Provided your insomnia is a new condition resulting from your breakup, you probably don't need to take sleep-inducing drugs. You need a plan.

Sleep Rules

The first phase of a good night's rest begins right now, with an assessment of your sleep tools. Are your mattress and pillow comfortable? Is the room in which you sleep dark and quiet enough to permit you to rest undisturbed? If not, fix these problems as soon as you can.

The next phase of a good night's sleep begins in the afternoon, when you avoid all drinks which contain caffeine. While most caffeine is flushed from your system within a few hours of ingestion, you may now be extra sensitive to its stimulating effects, so keep a ten hour interval between coffee- or tea-time and bedtime, to be safe.

You can use other foods to make you more ready to sleep. Tryptophan is an essential amino acid that has also proven to be a useful antidepressant. Tryptophan is also known to be useful as a sleep-enhancer. It's found in abundance in such foods as fish, turkey, chicken, cottage cheese, avocados, bananas and wheat-germ. So instead of warm milk and cookies, try some quacamole before bedtime. If you'd like, buy some melatonin tablets at a health food store and take one (why not, it's natural) along with your snack.

Always set aside enough rest time so that you

can wake up in the morning without using an alarm clock. Say good night to friends at least a half hour before bedtime, and begin your preparations for the relief that will follow.

Spend that last half hour outside of the bedroom. You want to teach your body to associate your bed only with sleep. Go to bed only when you're ready to sleep, and like Pavlov's dog, your body will soon respond by turning out your lights almost as soon as your head hits the pillow. If you are in the habit of turning on the TV set at the foot of your bed and watching until sleep overtakes you, break the habit. You'll find that you're less likely to wake up in the middle of the night if you do, and that going to sleep will happen more swiftly.

It's also best to go to bed and wake up at the same time of day, weekdays and weekends. That way, you're working in harmony with your body's clock.

Day 5 Self-Regard

Free To Be Real

A jail we make for ourselves out of golden threads is still a jail. If you couldn't trust yourself to be yourself with someone else, the real you wasn't there to be appreciated. And that means you couldn't be loved for yourself, nor find the freedom to express and enable all that you *could* be. While sacrifice can be a component of a healthy relationship, it shouldn't hobble your soul. You can dedicate your deepest love without having to sacrifice your identity.

The life-denying compromises people make for a lover can literally be deadly. Why do we do this? Because we're lonely or because we think our options are limited? Yet have you ever had times with your ex when you'd wake up in the middle of the night and feel so alone, and not know what to do about it? Did you conclude that you couldn't talk to your ex about the feeling, or that talk wouldn't help? If so, you may have been spending an awful lot of time with someone while basically being quite alone.

In simpler times, mating was idealized as something much prettier. Strangers' eyes met and caused hearts to beat faster; people knew the other was "The Right One For Me" – that was it. And many years later, that's the same story they tell you. But too often these days, eyes may meet, hearts may pound, and it really doesn't matter. How many times have your heard friends describe a new prospect by the size of his bank account or her 'supermodel' looks?

And then there's the issue of choice – so many prospects to choose from. Were you ever paralyzed by too many choices? Many people are. Today there are far more choices; perhaps they're better described as temptations. But if you look to business for rational systems for making choices, you may discover a very compelling choice-making model.

In business, for example, when one vendor is chosen over a competitor, the selection process is based on systematically weighted criteria which make it possible for a logical choice to be made. Contrast that process to relationship formation, where romantic tradition once dictated that choices must be powered almost solely by emotional engines, fueled by everything from odors to hand size.

But there's a newer, more rational process that's growing in popularity and it's methods are more like the decision-making systems used in business.

This pragmatic method for matching prospective lovers is evident in many computer-automated dating services and their Websites. This approach enables prospects to match with others based on a large number of specific criteria. Its users maintain that the method works, *if* both parties are honest about themselves. Now let's suppose you took your ex and yourself and placed yourself in the computer dating-service model. Would you have had enough factors in common to inspire introductions? Would you have had enough complementary differences to be seen as a balanced pairing?

In business, when a bad choice is made, those involved can analyze their mistakes in hope of redirecting their future efforts more productively. You must do the same thing after a relationship fails. You must honestly understand why it didn't work. Discovering that truth can be painful, but ultimately it's liberating. Once embraced, the truth fosters forgiveness and release of the past. You and your ex were unable to hold up your own ends of the relationship, so it dissolved. Unlike business, nobody got fired. You're now free to become who you truly are. And the more clearly you can manifest that, the more serenity you'll bring to life.

So why did your relationship end? As we've said, people in unhealthy relationships often lose their sense of self. All relationships entail sacrifices, but did you keep your head so low that you gave up your identity just to keep the peace? Did your deprivations include friends you loved but your ex couldn't stand, the way you wore your hair, a hobby you liked, or even a quirky little habit that always brought out the wrath of your former lover? But now do you see that you could have fixed things just by adjusting your rational manner of making romantic choices?

There's no need to analyze every nuance of your failed relationship to see the light. It's enough to just get a general idea of why you were incompatible, and then let it go. An unhealthy relationship is restriction, constriction and suffocation. A healthy relationship is an expansion – an adventure of selves collaborating in their personal enhancements. Elderly couples who've been happily married for ages can still stimulate each other spiritually. And grow. Without the freedom to be real, a part of you will remain stunted, confined, and unable to grow.

The intent of this day is to explore those buried pieces of yourself so you can bring them out and celebrate them. This is who you truly are! And in resurrecting these forgotten parts of yourself, you reduce your chances of being hurt again in the future.

The more of your own inner truth you can make available to the world, the more you'll attract people who will appreciate you for exactly who you are. Acceptance from others who truly matter begins with self-acceptance. No more apologizing for being who you are. No more hiding!

Sometimes we exit a relationship in great despair initially and then we begin to remember that we had a life before we ever knew our ex. It's a process of rediscovery, to get ourselves back on a good track once again.

Here's a simple exercise. Think of two or three things that your ex did or didn't do that made you feel bad about yourself. Reclaim these missing pieces of you, and vow to never again let them be buried. Do these things as much as you can for the next thirty days. Add to this list as you see fit.

TIP . . . Body Support

There's no better way to deal with your frustrations and pain than by getting some safe but stimulating physical exercise. If you haven't regularly worked out before but begin your recovery program with a new commitment to a regular exercise regimen, you can be well on your way to getting in shape by the time your first month is over.

Our first fitness recommendation is to see a doctor for counsel if you are over 35 and haven't been in shape for a while. Even if you're under 35 but have health risk conditions, ask your doctor to help you restore your fitness. Ask for whatever tests he or she feels may help you to work out a safe but progressive exercise plan. The following guidelines may help you design your plan. The President's Council on Physical Fitness and Sports originally developed them.

Why should you bother? Because fitness will increase your ability to deal with stress, make you more alert and emotionally at ease, serve as an outlet for your frustrated aggressions, let you sleep more soundly, and help restore your natural sense of confidence and peace with the world. In short, it will protect your health and improve your well-being.

How do you attain such a wonderful state? You know the answer: you work. Grunt and puff work. Also, you need to start eating right, to get your weight into a range that will make you even more attractive to your next great love, when the time is right. See our tips on diet for more on that. For the moment, let's focus on your body's total fitness.

Total fitness calls for work on four different areas of your physical capabilities. You want to increase your cardiovascular fitness, the strength of your muscles, your endurance, and your flexibility. To get where you need to be, you'll need to plan for three to four workouts a week, ideally one session every other day. Day, night or noon, whatever suits your schedule and pleases you most. The length of those workouts will vary with your age, fitness level, and ultimate goals. Fortunately, attaining simple health requires shorter workouts than getting the body of Adonis or Aphrodite.

The average person simply pursuing good health should begin each workout with a five to ten minute warm up. Include stretches to promote flexibility. Every workout should include a twenty minute oxygen-burning aerobic exercise (brisk walking, swimming, jogging, cycling, rowing, cross country skiing, skipping rope, or fast competitive games like handball or tennis) for your cardiovascular system. Then a 30 minute workout with weights for muscular development of all muscle groups and calisthenics for endurance should complete your workout. Then cool down for a few minutes with walking and stretches.

To play it safe, make sure that your cardiovascular workout doesn't exceed your abilities, especially at first. Use your heart rate as a guide to your limits. That means you must wear a watch or watch a clock while you work out. To get fit, you must keep your heart rate elevated but in a safe range for your age. There are several ways of calculating the heart rate you should maintain while you work out. An easy one is subtract your age from 220 and then multiply the result by 70%. Thus, the target workout heart rate for a 30 year-old would be 133. Take your pulse early and often while you work out, until you learn what rates your body can handle.

Exercise will also help you bring your weight

into a healthier balance between fatty tissue and muscle mass. Even chewing gum all the time can help you lose 10 pounds a year—provided that it's sugar free. Even a moderate half hour workout three times a week will burn off another ten pounds. And a vigorous workout will reset your body's metabolic rate to burn more calories for more than just the time you're at work.

Weather plays a role in your workouts as well. Remember to dress more lightly for outdoor exercise than you would if you were going out to relax. And it's not a good idea to workout in hot and humid weather, or on a full stomach, no matter what your age or condition.

Okay, we've told you what's best for you. But you're one of those people who won't face up to the need to reform your couch potato ways. At least try to change the way you live to include a little more action than before. Do things like climbing a few flights of stairs instead of taking the escalator, plan on longer walks from your bus or parked car, take a walk instead of or at least with your midday snacks, carry your own baggage, and so forth.

Any change that puts you more into motion is better than nothing at all.

Day 6 — Solitude

The Price You Pay

Breakups don't want for extremes. It's often all blame or all shame. "It's all his fault" or "it's all my fault." Or "if only I had done this or that differently." And "the end" often happens several times before it actually takes hold. That may take extra time, but for some it's a very good way to evolve out of a relationship.

Breakups can happen coldly, or even brutally. One or both parties can suffer severe emotional injuries as a result – injuries that can linger for months or years. This condition used to provide an extended gravy train for psychotherapists who could spend all the many months required to help their clients heal their psychic wounds.

As people came to increasingly depend on managed care to pay their mental health bills, more of these love-wounded warriors fell into file folders under a benefits management schedule. Instantly their therapists had to get them all recovered within five sessions because that's when the insurance coverage runs dry.

So how good is your insurance coverage?

The shock-period immediately following a

breakup can be the most dangerous part of the letting-go process. It's a time when you want to beat yourself or your ex-lover up. You'll try to imagine what it all could have been like if only you could rewind the clock and be just a bit different in this way or that. Most people know that it's foolish to live under an umbrella of guilt and shame. But there's a problem: Once you begin to beat yourself up, it's hard to stop. You could well wind up doing it over and over again. You master the ugly art of wasting emotional time.

It may seem that if you keep reviewing the same material, it's going to somehow make all the pain go away. Buddhists chant repetitive mantras to focus their minds on emptiness. But if that same Buddhist turns her anxieties into repetitious reviews, her woes too would deepen. Like any pest, the more we encourage our pains, the longer they hang around.

Some pairs of lovers are just plain comfortable with each other. Other couples keep each other on their toes. Either way can be okay. But if you're bored, then you may have a problem. Boredom does *not* induce sleepiness. It may cause conflict, but fighting only partly relieves boredom. It can be expected whenever one party to a pairing refuses to mature and evolve. The same familiar habits become boring rather than endearing, the same old issues get stale. Both boredom and conflict are signs that it's time for a fundamental relationship review. If it proves to be time to part, it doesn't matter who finally announces the end of the relationship – you can't kill what's dead, you can only have the common-sense to acknowledge it.

In your arguments, you're likely to feel that you were never truly heard or understood by your ex. You may still want your ex to hear your pleas. You may have had emergency backslides, you may even still want to go back and rewrite history. It's only natural.

If you do reach for the phone, be fair to yourself first: Remember beforehand that, yes, moving on *can* be painful. But at the same time it could enormously enrich you, at the very least with a far better self-understanding. These considerations may help to remind you of why you concluded that it was time to move on.

If you successfully resist the temptation to pick up the phone, take stock, right now. Look how far you've come in dealing with your pain and recovery in just a few days. Remember that you're unlikely to feel any worse than you do right now. In short, you're probably in better shape than you expected to be just a few days ago. And in just a few more weeks, you should feel a LOT better than you do now.

TIP . . . The Stress Yardstick

Of course you're not imagining the pain you now feel. It's quite real. The pain caused by the end of the central love relationship in your life can be one of the most stressful events you can experience. Do you need to take immediate action to prevent the stress of your break-up from making you sick, or even worse? There's a logical, objective way to answer this question.

We must credit Doctors T H Holmes and R H Rahe for the answer, in the form of their Social Readjustment Scale. This scale identifies a broad range of factors that create stress in one's life. Better yet, it assigns a number of 'Life Crisis Units (LCUs) to each of these different events, based on the degree of stress each factor causes the average person. Sure, it's an oversimplification, but it does provide you with one very important insight: a way to assess the degree of risk your current situation poses to your health as well as your emotional well-being.

Here's how to use this idea: examine the following table and total up the LCUs for the life crises that you've experienced in the past two years. If you total over 300 LCUs for that span of time, your probability of illness is said to be over 80%. If your LCUs range between two hundred and three hundred, your odds of an illness are 50%. If your LCUs are between 150 and 200, your odds of an illness are one in three.

Now, this is very important. This chart does not mean you *will* get sick. But it does in fact, show the genuine corollaries between stressful events and their potential to affect your health. Here's the chart:

Event	Life Cycle Units
Death of spouse	100
Divorce	73
Separation	65
Jail term	63
Death of close family member	63
Personal illness or injury	53
Marriage	50
Fired at work	47
Marital reconciliation	45
Retirement	45
Change in health of family member	44
Pregnancy	40
Sex difficulties	39

Gain of new family member	39
Business readjustment	38
Change in financial state	38
Death of close friend	37
Change to a different line of work	36
Increase in arguments with spouse	35
A large mortgage or loan	30
Foreclosure of mortgage or loan	30
Change in responsibilities at work	29
Son or daughter leaving home	29
Trouble with in-laws	29
Outstanding personal achievement	28
Spouse begins or stops work	26
Begin or end of school or college	26
Change in living conditions	25
Change in personal habits	24
Trouble with boss	23
Change in work hours or conditions	20
Change in residence	20
Change in school or college	20
Change in recreation	19
Change in church activities	19
Change in social activities	18
A moderate loan or mortgage	17
Change in sleeping habits	16
Changed no. of family gatherings	15
Change in eating habits	15
Holiday	13
Christmas	12
Minor violations of the law	11

Life *without* stress can be bland to insipid, but too much stress can kill you. Even if you're young and in good health, the pressures of too many stressful events can lead people to highly dangerous escapist behavior. Overuse of drugs or alcohol, or resorting to careless sexual encounters can pose dramatic risks to your health and well-being. These "escapes" will afford you little real relief from the pressures you face.

If you find yourself approaching a high-risk status on the Life Crisis Units stress-o-meter, it's time to put yourself on a strict stress budget. Put off changing jobs or moving, at least for a while. Let things settle down in your life before you take on more challenges. And be sure to pursue health and wellness as vigorously as you can. Eat right and exercise.

Most importantly, understand that there is a way to come through these hard feelings. There is always a way. For more tips on stress management and reduction, see the Internet at http://www.psychwww.com/mtsite/smlcu.html and http://www.psychwww.com/mtsite/smpage.html

Day 7 Values

The Ideal Lover

No matter how much you may hurt today, you'll be shedding your pain and moving on, probably sooner than you now believe possible. So even though it may now sound distasteful or unlikely, you will someday have to decide whether you wish to find someone else with whom you can share an intimate love.

Incidentally, the odds are good that if you're reading this book, you aren't yet ready to launch your new love-prospect screening program. If you're still hurting from the loss of your last lover, it will take you a while to recharge the emotional batteries that will permit you to whole-heartedly share yourself with someone new.

Worse, if you try to do that right now, you face even better odds that your rebound affair will almost certainly bring you no sustaining satisfaction. Even if your fling just gives you the chance to revenge yourself on your ex, it's still an affair that looks to your past, not your future.

However, it's *not* too soon to begin to consider the right and the wrong way to go about finding a love-mate. If for no other reason, these considerations can

help you to better understand why your last relationship didn't work out.

So what's it like to be "a single" today?

A leading online dating service recently sur-
veyed thousands of members. Over three-quarters of
the participants said that the dates they met through
the service were nothing at all like the way these dates
had described themselves in the service's portfolios. So
what does this mean? Are people better at deception
than at courtship and intimacy?

It could be that the majority of people who form
new relationships really don't have a clear picture of
what they're seeking. Or it could mean that people
don't really know how others see them. Or they do, and
are afraid that others won't find their packaging very
attractive.

Unfortunately, many people still seem to entertain a sixth-grade fairy-tale fantasy of who their unique
Mr. or Ms Right ought to be. She's a true Goddess fresh
from the froth of Sports Illustrated's swimwear edition.
He's a knight (with a large estate) in sparkling armor,
riding to her rescue; naturally, she'll never have to work
again. As the dating service survey shows, in order to
appeal to such paragons, people will often resort to lies
or self-deception.

What is your ideal lover like? Have you really
thought critically about your own fantasies or are you
still hanging on to sophomoric notions? And once
they've selected their others, some people become
addicted to these lovers. Much has been written about
how the female hormone oxytocin plays a mediating

role in romances. For some women it may even create a virtual addiction to an intimate relationship. Researchers have claimed that this may be why women can require more time to recover from a breakup than men. Unfortunately for them, most studies have shown that men take longer to truly recover but move on more quickly.

At the moment, your picture of your ideal lover is still likely to resemble the person from whom you've just parted. That's understandable. When breakups occur, the loss leaves a hole; people miss the other person and may even long for them. So it's natural to conclude that your ex must have been your ideal lover.

But today, you can rise above the sixth-grade level of thinking. Think of how much you have already discovered about yourself in just the past few days. Now you can rethink your ideal lover. What would that person be like? Start your imagining by thinking well of yourself, well enough to be willing to be loved in all of the ways you truly want to be loved. That means know who you are, admitting both your faults and your glories. In light of that clarity, create a new, clearer picture of who you truly want to love.

Using your new-found clarity, once you begin to seek a new love you'll find yourself saying "no thank-you" to the ones who don't fit, who won't make you happy, and "maybe" to those who seem to possess the traits you're going to be looking for.

Think about the traits you're really looking for, or were looking for before your ex came along. Did fear of ending up alone take you away from your last search for a lover? Loneliness is a terrible motivator. But without negative influences holding you back, your possibilities will considerably expand.

Imagine that it's time to begin looking again. Who would you really want as a lover? What kind of person would you now like to welcome into your life? Let's create a fantasy of what you truly want. Think of an ideal lover in realistic terms. Forget all the material issues. Imagine the specifics of someone whose character and integrity you can really trust and love:

What is it about this person that you would find most attractive? Why are these features important to you now?

If one of you doesn't dance, that's not going to ruin the relationship. But if you have in common some important values and have complementary differences, if you appreciate each other's stories and struggles, share laughter and even tears, it's safe to say you enjoy a very positive attraction.

See that lover in your mind. Let the image and personality become familiar. Observe how much this ideal mate differs from your ex. Now ask yourself: why you didn't pursue someone like this a long time ago? What has prevented you from having the love you wanted and truly deserved?

Someday, if or when you can renew your interest in relationships, your ideal lover may yet await you. Perhaps, though, they're not waiting on a white horse or in a designer swimsuit. Will an old white Mustang do instead? Yes, you can change your values. So don't turn a deaf ear when opportunity knocks.

💡TIP . . . Reason Trumps Feelings

We grant that repressed feelings can be the source of secret pain and consequent evil. However, the currently fashionable emphasis on the importance of feelings may have led to a popular misconception, that emotions should be the primary determinant of one's actions, rather than reason.

The great psychoanalyst Carl Jung stressed that people experience the world in four ways:

- with their intellects
- with their emotions
- with their sensations, and…
- with their intuitions.

Well balanced individuals will use all four of these faculties together in order to deal effectively with the reality of their circumstances. On the other hand, someone whose behavior is controlled purely by emotions will usually be seen as having problems with impulse control, emotional maturity, or socialization skills.

Another psychotherapist, Nathaniel Branden, claimed that our emotions start in infancy as simply pleasure or pain. We learn to associate one or the other with all of our experiences. Over time, we learn to call a certain kind of pleasure "love," or another kind "laughter." And we learn to call one pain "hot" while another may be "sharp" or "sad." Gradually, we build up a whole spectrum of feelings that can even combine pleasure and pain (forget sadomasochism; do you like hot food? Or getting tickled?).

Branden also says that when we learn to associate a kind of experience with a particular feeling it produces, you can say that we have formed a "value" about the thing that provoked the feeling. Do you look forward to a roller coaster ride? Then you positively value it. Do you fear roller coaster rides? Then you negatively value them.

Stick with us just a bit more on this, because it's about to get real important: Branden then says that feelings result from our subconscious mind producing an almost instantaneous summary of all of experiences with the thing we are about to react to. This summary is a physical expression of our values in reaction to the thing that causes us to react. Show me a snarling cocker spaniel, and nearly at the speed of light, I feel the sense of rage and frustration that I felt at age seven when a friend's pet cocker bit me, and I couldn't respond by biting him back (after all, my friend's Mom was sitting right there).

What's the point? It's simply this: Branden next tells us, correctly, that it's not possible to use just your will to change your feelings about things. Try as you might, you can't wish away the pain you may feel about the loss of a lover.

But here's the silver lining offered by Branden's psychology. He teaches that while we can't change our feelings, we can change our values, by using our minds to review them and establish new priorities, new values. I'll never be able to force myself to feel that cocker spaniels are anything but overbred hairballs. But if I think hard enough about their redeeming qualities, I will ultimately be able to forgive and forget. Or even to establish a new positive regard for the breed.

All by using the power of the mind, not to coerce or control feelings (which is a total waste of time, anyway), but to modify them in keeping with thoughtful reflection and reordering of one's personal values.

Reason trumps feelings, given enough time.

Are you hurt and angry right now? What values have produced those feelings? A sense of loss of someone you loved? Feelings of hurt and anger at having been betrayed? Emotions of fear and despair because you feel you've been forced to betray someone you once loved? All of these feelings of woundedness can be more rapidly healed if you find new values for those things that are causing you pain.

Do you still value your ex? Do you realistically expect that you will feel the same way about him or her in ten more years? How are you likely to value this person at that far-distant time? What's to prevent you from changing the way you value that person now, to the same values you will feel for them a decade from now?

"Hey, remember good old whatsizname?"

Day 8 Perspective

Missing Time

How amazing: you've already come through your first week on your own, and you've already had some good moments as well as bad. But hopeful signs don't mean you're going to suddenly stop missing your ex. Perhaps you'll even be tempted to toss this book aside, pick up the phone, and call to see if you can go running back to your old familiar pains instead of dealing with this new loneliness.

But if you know that the relationship is over, those impulses will dissipate. By now, you're beginning to see your ex from a different perspective. Missing someone can make you forget why you parted. Go back and in a very short time, you may well say, "Oh y-e-e-e-a-h! THAT'S why I left." You may well recall some of the happy moments you spent together. But you're also likely to remember the price you paid for those good times.

The following exercise will help relieve your fleeting pains of loss and any impulse you might have to accommodate your ex for the sake of a reconciliation, even at an exorbitant price:

Think of what you miss the most. Now, compare that to the answer to this question: Were you addicted to someone who failed to give you what you needed? Then, think about the price you had to pay. Think about the few pleasantries you accepted in exchange for being made to feel bad or doubtful about yourself.

The next time you miss your former lover, or when you're feeling tired or sad, turn to this page and say "Yes, I miss my ex because of the sweet little things, but I also remember the price I paid. And that price was and always will be, too high!

If you face such temptations, they can be more painful than your initial sense of loss. The temptation makes it hard to stand tall. But the more you stand your rightful ground, the happier you'll eventually be.

You don't need to be anybody's victim if you choose not to be. But someone who knows how to push your buttons can still manipulate the wounds from your recent parting. Missing your former lover hurts. But a personal commitment to move through it with dignity and honor can eventually leave you with more pride and serenity than you've ever known.

♀TIP . . . Happy Meals

Who needs diets? Ending a relationship can be the most effortless weight loss program you never asked for. Dramatic loss of weight is a common result of the stresses brought on by the end of a core relationship. Loss of appetite, being awake and burning calories for more sleepless hours per day, and important dietary changes are the usual causes. If these changes aren't remedied, they can amplify a slide into depression or even more severe, life-threatening medical conditions.

So protect yourself from the impact of these stresses. Defend yourself with good nutrition. Here are some pointers for restorative eating.

Chocoholicism: No Sin

Be of good cheer, you chocoholics. The rumors are true: chocolate can actually help improve your mood. First, cocoa contains a natural chemical (anandamide) which stimulates the same area in the brain that marijuana does. Don't worry, though. One expert calculates that if you weigh 130 pounds, you'd have to gobble up 25 pounds of chocolate to get a buzz.

Second, chocolate helps your brain make opioids, opium-like chemicals that dull pain and produce a slightly euphoric feeling.

Third, chocolate also has a chemical related to amphetamines (phenylethylamine) that has been called "the love-drug." It helps to lower blood pressure, speed up your pulse, and makes blood-sugar levels rise. Caffeine in chocolate may also increase your alertness. But again, don't worry: another expert says you'd have to eat more than 12 Hershey bars to get a caffeine kick equal to a single cup of coffee.

But hold off on buying yourself a box of your favorite chocolate candies. Chocolate is best consumed as a Mexican-style molé sauce served over chicken, or in a glass of lightly sweetened cocoa before bedtime. The warm milk should help you get to sleep, naturally.

Carbos And Vitamins You Need

Your brain needs a chemical called serotonin to properly regulate your mood. When your body whips up a good batch of serotonin, you feel good. And if you go without it for very long, you may feel depressed. How can you be sure your body can make enough of this happy stuff? Get 40% to 60% of your calories from such complex carbohydrates as fruits and vegetables, dairy products, beans, grains and cereals. And avoid the insulin roller coaster, and abrupt energy and mood swings, which eating sugars, even fruit sugar (fructose) in juices or soft drinks, can cause.

For our part, we like to avoid the toxicity of artificial sweeteners, too; once you lose your sweet tooth, you may even find your thinking becoming clearer, as your too-common systemic yeast infection (candidiasis) dies off.

You want to avoid dietary deficiencies that have been linked to conditions of depression. That means you should take dietary supplements that contain B-complex vitamins, particularly folic acid, thiamin, riboflavin, niacin and B6. We encourage you to also take 2,000 mg of the amino acid 1-tyrosine in the morning. You can find it in most health food stores. If you really want to play it safe, ask your doctor to prescribe a perfectly safe Tryptophan supplement such as Optimax, and take 2,000 mg at bedtime. Or have three ounces of turkey breast every night before retiring.

Avoid caffeine drinks past noon; you need your rest. Try not to drink more than one cup of "high-test" coffee per day. As for alcohol: limit yourself to no more than one drink per day, preferably taken at least four hours before bedtime. It's too easy to begin to use the stuff as a crutch; why risk it? And if you are inclined to feel depressed, avoid any use of alcohol.

The Virtues Of Fat

Americans are currently oversold on the idea that all fat in the diet is bad. Granted, excess dietary or body fat can cause heart disease and some forms of cancer. But more often than not, if you are overweight, it's because you eat too many simple carbohydrates, and the wrong *kinds* of fat.

Believe it or not, some kinds of dietary fat are essential. You need to eat them or die, or at least run serious risks to your mental health. After all, your brain is mostly fatty tissue. To stay in a good mood, you must eat enough of the right kinds of fat. That includes Omega-3 fatty acids from plants, nuts, and seeds, and EPA and DHA from oils found in seafood. If you can't stand fish, get some EPA tablets from a health food store and take a couple of gelcaps every day.

The Herbal Pharmacopoeia

If you think you're getting seriously depressed, see your doctor for prescription medications. Short of such a serious conclusion, consider the use of herbs to buoy up your spirits.

One herb, St. Johns' wort (Hypericum perforatum) has received considerable media attention of late. They say that it has antibacterial, antiviral, and antifungal effects, and that drinking two or three cups a day of its tea can cure some cases of depression and chronic fatigue syndrome within a month. It contains a chemical known as SAM-e, short for S-adenosyl-l-methionine.

SAM-e is a chemical your body produces from an amino acid methionine, that is believed to boost the happy brain chemical serotonin. Taking 1600 mg of this herb a day produced positive results for 61% of depressed people in a three-week study in Europe. That was slightly better than the 59% of those whose depressed condition improved thanks to taking Tofranil, a prescription antidepressant.

However, extended use may cause kidney and bladder damage, and high levels of sun sensitivity. Check with your doctor if you are using any prescription medications. St. Johns' wort can cause nasty reactions with narcotics, diet pills, asthma medications, decongestants, and amphetamines.

Other antidepressant herbs include pleasant tasting Lemon Balm, which can also be used as a sedative. Licorice and common sage (Salvia officinalis) are also believed to have antidepressant effects. Teas made with the herb sage can help quickly restore emotional balance in the face of panic or stress reactions.

Isn't it wonderful that nature provides all these painlessly natural ways to ease the pain of a loss like yours?

Trust School

This is your day to explore the issues of trust. We'll review the degree of mistrust that you feel for your ex. And let's consider how you can rediscover sufficient trust to maintain other healthy relationships.

Let's start this inquiry by recognizing an ugly truth: Often the real causes of mistrust reflect back on ourselves. If you were never willing to trust your ex completely, why were you surprised when your ex proved to be untrustworthy?

Said another way, people you trust will sometimes prove worthy of that trust, but people whose motives you suspect will almost *always* prove worthy of your mistrust. In short, due caution is healthy but unwarranted wariness is a guaranteed relationship-killer.

You miss the love you once had, the comfort you once enjoyed. But isn't it possible that you miss what never was? And once your trust or faithfulness was truly breached, there may not *be* a real relationship. But it's easy to get confused as to who really broke faith with whom. It's almost like asking who stopped loving whom first? Trust doesn't just mean loyalty. It can imply sustainability, reliability, and decency.

Mistrust is born when a shared understanding, spoken, written, or just assumed (like common courtesy), is violated. Acts like temper tantrums, holding the relationship hostage, sudden cancellation of expected emotional expressions can all do the deed.

Unwillingness to trust another seems to be at the root of contemporary relationship breakups and breakdowns as often as the more commonly told tales of betrayals. So we live in an age of suspicion, of love held hostage to failed hopes. Too often, it's a case of "guilty before proven innocent." People say that they want to have a loving covenant but let their relationships fail from having no real foundation of positive intention.

It was simpler when you couldn't trust someone in a relationship if they were unfaithful, and unfaithful meant only that they went out and had a secret dalliance with someone else. The term "unfaithful" in today's relationships means something different. It now seems to mean what it says: "no faith." No faith that a loving relationship can work, or that two people can rise above and surmount any and all challenges, present ones and especially ones that are long-passed.

Relationships without trust usually amount to nothing but a manipulative co-dependency. They're like Shakespeare's tangled web, in that a couple of people don't want to be alone so they settle for less than either party wants. But since no one's happy in the relationship both parties wind up wishing they were alone. In the meantime, they secretly wish they could be with someone they truly love, and who would welcome their love in return. But since trust is so hard to come by for these people, they settle for less than they want, and then wonder why their love life is in shambles.

Sound familiar?

If you want to trust someone, especially in a new love relationship someday, trust that they will be just as humanly frail as you, and make mistakes just like you do. But most importantly, trust that their intentions are inspired by love. To have this opportunity, this strength, you'll need to commit to the happy, hopeful uncertainty of the future from right here in the past. This will help return you to your true and loving ideals and will return your body, mind, and soul to a true center.

If you need some experience with this kind of trust, practice it with strangers. Tell the next new acquaintance you speak with something about yourself that you would normally conceal. Tell them something that you genuinely feel ashamed of, or dislike about yourself, or are still embarrassed to confess. You are likely to be astonished to find that taking a chance on this kind of self-disclosure makes other people want to protect you, in gratitude for your having exposed your vulnerability to them.

Like they say, love makes the world go 'round…

 **TIP . . . Water Works**

Among the many things that promote healing is water. The first thing we do with a wound is to wash it. So whether a cool drink or a soothing aromatherapy bath, we urge you to seek aquatic consolation whenever you can.

Why is water so useful? It's not just a matter of it being the dominant chemical found in our bodies. It's not even that we are conceived and spend the first nine months of our lives floating in a water-filled sac. It could well be even deeper than that: racial memories, if you will. We have a hunch that those who say we evolved from a simian species that lived by the sea-shore are right. We've kept too many vestigial remnants of our watery past to be a coincidence. Our hairless bodies, the webs between our fingers and thumbs, the way we have sex face to face, the shapes of our down-ward pointing noses and the way our lungs and breath-ing apparatus respond to immersion in water, all are signs that we were designed to work well in the water.

Perhaps that's why many psychologists remark on the sea being seen as a subconscious symbol of nurture and wholeness in dreams.

What To Do?

Because water is a special element for mankind, you can find comfort in using it in a number of ways. This comfort will help you to heal the wound of your loss. Here are some of the things you can do to use water to wash yourself emotionally clean.

1.   Take solace in the shower. Do it at least daily, not only for the simple ritual of cleaning your skin and hair, but for the sensory indulgence of feeling it pour over your skin. Feel the temperature of the water on the back of your neck. That's where your body's thermostat is set. Let warm water pour over the spot at the base of the back of your neck, and you'll emerge feeling warm in the coldest weather. Or run cool water there, and feel at ease when it's hotter than Phoenix.

2.   Take a steam bath. Use the facilities at your

local gym or health club, or get friends to invite you as a guest to theirs. It's a great way to cleanse your system of a whole bunch of toxins, and then you can again enjoy the act of taking a shower to rinse off.

3. For a real treat, soak in a tub. Make the water as hot as you can take it, and then ease into a feeling of increasingly penetrating relaxation of every muscle that enrobes your body. If you can, use a hot tub for your soak. There's nothing more invigorating than the energetic swirling of the currents in these devices. It's a sensory treat without any need for sexual spice. And even if you're supposed to be an adult, if you're alone, why not use bubble bath or a nice scented oil to make the sensory indulgence of your whole experience even richer?

4. Look in the Yellow Pages and see if you can find a place that offer floatation tanks. These remarkable devices contain a shallow pool of skin-temperature water that's been loaded with Epsom salts. The water's so heavy your body will easily float with a low water line. If you can find a rental facility, you'll go in and spend an hour in the light-tight tank floating in water that you soon lose track of as water. You will wind up feeling like you're floating in space, or nowhere at all. It can be the most profoundly relaxing experience you'll ever have in your life.

5. Go for a swim. It's a great way to work out for both aerobic and developmental benefits. And you'll run very little risk of overstressing any muscle group with excess exertions. This time when you swim, notice everything about how you breathe as you enter the water, and how the water feels on your skin from first immersion to the time you return to the ground.

6.   And finally, don't forget to wrap yourself around at least eight twelve-ounce glasses of water or water-bearing beverages a day. Good hydration will help you to purify your system, and stay well nourished. If you find yourself drinking fluids less often than this, have at least one sixteen ounce serving of something, once every three hours of the day. If you must, force yourself. Water's that important to your health and feelings of well-being.

Day 10 — Identity

Celebration of Self

Fear is a prison. Whatever you fear rules you, just like a bad relationship can rule you. You always have the power and the right to rise above your fears. But you don't feel that power right now, do you?

You know there's something special about you. It's that specialness that let you connect with your ex when you first met. But somehow, that part of you got buried as you struggled to find happiness in a relationship that was no longer life enhancing.

There are satisfactions that motivate the care that maintains a happy, healthy relationship: we get companionship, support, care, mutual nurturing. We feed a healthy relationship from our heart with our love. We are rewarded by the return of that love. A good relationship's potential for growth is only limited by our potential for caring.

But when a relationship sours, it becomes boring and tedious. Hope and care are replaced with fear: fear of unpleasant feelings about a once beloved mate, and a longing to be elsewhere. *Anywhere* else. And of course, as a result, you feel alone.

Loneliness is a terrible motivator. If you don't

deal with it appropriately, it can lock you into a frozen inertia. You may get lost in your unhealthy relationship. There, you may forget who you are. Once you fail to recognize your own true self, you might then delude yourself into believing that being by yourself is tantamount to being nothing in a nowhere place. Almost like death, in miniature form.

That's the worst aspect of an unhealthy relationship, the risk of forgetting who you really are. And the longer you linger in nowhere, getting and giving nothing at all, the more you forget yourself. No wonder people feel weakened, diminished and unable to love again after an experience like that.

So it stands to reason that if you learn to stand strong within your own true self, you won't require an excessively long time to heal from the wounds of a negative relationship.

Standing strong, remembering who you truly are, is a process that can begin at any time. It's simply a matter of making a decision to do so. And the sooner you take this step, the sooner you can see where you truly are in any relationship. So what happens if you rediscover yourself while you're within a relationship and then find that you and your mate are worlds apart?

The sooner you know, the sooner you'll grow. Together, or apart.

The feeling of emptiness that results from such a discovery is completely understandable. But once a dead relationship has been mercifully put to sleep, why do you still feel so inconsolable? The reason may not be clear to you. In fact, you may have buried or repressed your own power for so long a time that you feel incapable of moving on without the strength and support of a lover, even the lover you just left behind. Or who left you.

What a paradox – you think you require strength and support from another, even the very person that you're now trying to flee. Let's say you ask for your ex's advice and counsel, thinking that you need them to feel a bit more whole. But even if you get good, sound advice it has little value, because it doesn't come from the greater wisdom within you. And until it does, until you're willing to scrape away your confusion and self-doubt, you'll fail to rediscover the full extent of your own real value. Your choices will be based upon a self-repressed sense of who you truly are and can grow to become at any time in your life.

Fix this. All you have to do is take a little time to honestly assess your own strengths and weaknesses, accept them, and celebrate all of those things that make you special, unique and yet universally human. And then rejoice in your freedom, and your ability to accept responsibility for the conduct and contents of all of your life.

Do you need years to do this? Some therapists might still insist that you do. But before you accept that as gospel, try the following simple exercise. And if you're able to complete it within a day or so, you've proven that you already know these important truths about yourself. It's entirely possible that you do, because even in an uncomfortable relationship, you are with yourself all of the time. The way you feel about things, the way you react to them tells you the truth about who you really are.

Work through the following exercise and begins this important step of reacquainting yourself with yourself.

Think of at least ten wonderfully special things about yourself. Start by figuring out...

What makes you smile?

What do people most like about you?

What is your kindest trait?

What is your strongest trait?

What is your goofiest side?

What can you do that nobody else can?

How do you show people you love them?

For the next ten days, think about one of these traits before you go to sleep. Before you're tempted to regress, turn your current situation into the most joyous place you can possibly create.

TIP ... Keep In Touch

It's a strange fact about being human: we need to be touched by others of our kind. For adults, the need is a subtle one, one we can defer at will. But the need is so urgent for new humans that infants have been consistently reported to shrivel and even die without the regular touch of another person. Even if it's contact of the most uncaring kind. So what do you do when a break-up occurs? The one person you depended on for physical intimacy, for just simple touching, is now out of your life.

Most Americans have never been very comfortable with casual physical contact, aside from a brief handshake of greeting. And now political correctness may actually make this physically isolating situation worse. Many people now fear that offering a person in your circumstances an uninvited touch of consolation may be misinterpreted as a predatory advance. So your sense of physical isolation may grow more pronounced as an unfortunate consequence of this climate.

This untouchable isolation is what leads many people to fall into the trap of trying to use promiscuity as a consolation device, only to find that it makes their sense of emptiness more profound. The problem with sex on the rebound doesn't lie in the search for intimacy. Usually the real problem is that a person in the early stages of grief and recovery isn't usually ready to make a meaningful and satisfying sexual connection with anyone new for a matter of months after an important relationship ends.

So you are still faced with the need for physical contact that will give you a tactile sense of your own skin, and even of being valued as a person. What can you do about this?

Start by taking charge. Make it a fun game. See how many people you can touch in a day, or get to touch you in a satisfying, positive way. And remember that everyone is just like you. They need to be touched, too. So in reaching out to others to obtain their touching, you'll be doing their mental health a little bit of good, too.

How can you appropriately secure the kind of contact you need without inviting people to take advantage of your vulnerability or accuse you of political incorrectness? Simple: start by being honest and open about what you want… and don't want, with everyone.

Ask for a hug from those people who you can trust to not sexualize matters. That includes platonic friends of your own gender (yes, it's okay for straight guys to hug each other now), brothers and other family members, even business acquaintances of the opposite sex who won't feel awkward or get out of line. If you're unsure about the degree to which you can trust someone to understand your invitation, keep the hug down to a simple cheek-to-cheek, upper-body-arm-wrap exchange. Save full body length contacts for those who won't think twice about what you intend.

Whenever it seems appropriate, shake hands like a gifted politician does, using both hands. Grip the other person's right hand with your right, while holding their arm or their shoulder with your left. Enjoy the greater sense of warmth this conveys, and the closeness this small extra move can engender.

We've lost the habit of doing anything more than greeting our co-workers with a nod and a smile in the morning, so try out some touching alternatives. Touch a same gendered person of equal rank on the shoulder in greeting, or as a reward for behavior you favor.

And if you can afford it, or perhaps even if you can't, at least once try getting a massage from a professional masseuse. You may even be able to arrange to have one come to your office or your home. Or check with your local sports center or health club to see if they offer this service to non-members or guests. A good, bracing massage followed by a bracing hot shower or steam bath can be among the most revitalizing of touching experiences.

And best of all, you'll be able to say when you're done: "look, mom: there was no sex to it at all."

Day 11 Reconnection

Recovering From 'Keep Away'

Yesterday, we discussed the most valuable component of your recovery-support system – your firm sense of yourself, your history and needs. As you grow to reclaim your genuine identity, your newly expanded self-awareness will help you to reclaim long-neglected friends and relatives as well.

What happens to all those people you once were so close to? How did you drift apart? Will they ever welcome you back? Yes, no, and maybe. Most real friends will understand. Your return to their fold will often come as a welcome relief. With others, perhaps you'll have to make amends for your neglect. Perhaps you can honestly explain that you were compromised by the feelings of your ex. Family members may take longer to forgive you if they resent your neglect, or even if they just disapprove of the end of your relationship.

Caring relatives can be an important asset for your recovery process. The right relative who has known you for a large part of your lifetime may have valuable perceptions about you. Some of these perceptions may be painful, especially now that you're raw from your loss. But if you trust the judgment and good will of your source, thank them for the courage they show in sharing their honest if hurtful insights. You need to value critical comments quite highly. Too often, such wisdom is passed along only when your back is turned. If you can accept them and change in response, it can help you to avoid falling into the same emotional potholes once again.

Make a list of ten good friends or close relatives that you haven't spoken to in too long a while. Then dig up and list their telephone numbers:

Call each one of the people on your list within the next two weeks. To the extent that you can avoid it, don't discuss your ex. Just recall and act on your best feelings for each of these loved ones. In the process, you'll probably also rediscover large parts of your own goodness and value. That will help to fill any number of the empty places in your heart.

 **. . . Get 'Stoned'**

Feelings aren't limited to your emotions alone. Every sense you have informs your body of the totality of your feelings. Whenever grief or sadness overtakes you, one way to ease your pain is to divert your attention to one of your senses which is having a pleasant experience.

For example, your sense of touch. Touch has feelings, too.

A Touching Tool For Stress

How do you arrest the attention of your sense of touch whenever you'd like? You might wish to buy a patented stress-relieving device over the Internet. It sells for $30, and is called the "Symphony of Palms TouchForm™." Many people report that it's a great way to reduce anxieties of all kinds. The device consists of nothing more than a palm-sized, flat piece of wood cut into a rounded shape, with a shallowly rounded, meandering groove cut into its face.

Users simply palm the thing and attentively run their finger around the groove. The inventor claims that the calm this produces requires less effort than meditation, and that "touch automatically and effortlessly focuses your mind, allowing it to let go of unwanted thoughts." The inventor also believes that part of the reason the device works is due to its use of "natural" materials.

Economy Class Tools

How would you like to save $29.50 on the price of a Symphony of Palms TouchForm? As an alternative, we don't suggest the use of Greek Worry Beads; too Sixties. Instead, head down to your nearest lawn and garden retailer. Look for the bins where they sell rocks that can be used as decorative accents in flowerbeds and pools. Find a nice, palm-sized oval black rock that has been washed by river water into a smoothness that your fingers find appealing. If the rock happens to have a groove that your fingers can follow around its surface, so much the better.

Buy that rock. It won't cost much, but it's about to become your constant companion.

Whenever you think of anything that makes you sad or anxious, reach into your pocket or purse for your friendly rock. If you want to give your rock a name, that's a good idea, too. It will make your friends smile indulgently when they see you pull out Rocky and begin to stroke its face.

You'll be amazed at how much peace and comfort that touching your rock's familiar surface will bring. But why stop with just touch?

Gold Plating Your Rocks

Your rock can bring you even more sensory pleasure, through your nose as well as your hands. It's easy to do. Just get some essential oils with a fragrance you like (or see our tips on "aromatherapy") and dilute them with alcohol. Don't use rubbing alcohol, use vodka instead. Then soak your rock overnight in this solution, or in a cologne that you like to wear. A porous rock will absorb enough of the scent overnight to provide you with a refreshing lift whenever you hold the rock under your nose.

You'd also be well advised to make or buy a small fabric bag with a drawstring closure in which you can keep your scented stone. That way, your purse or pocket won't give off an odor that other people might notice. Better yet, have your rock's bag made from velvet, and lined with an oil-resistant vinyl material. That way, you can enjoy yet another tactile experience as you touch your velvet-robed stone for the comfort and peace this feeling will give you.

Day 12 Peace

Panic Beater

Yes, time is your healer. But time's also likely to deliver unpleasant surprises. Some of the least pleasant events that may follow a breakup are abrupt fits of panic. Panic happens when you sense you're trapped. No one to fight with, nowhere to run. Trapped alone in the dark, lost and frightened. All you can see is the stark void of what's missing, while desperately fearing that the future only holds worse.

One of the hardest things to do in a faltering relationship is to see things logically, just as they are. And often, even if you can peer through the haze, it doesn't seem to matter. That's the bizarre thing about love versus logic. You may clearly perceive that someone isn't right for you, or may not even be faithful. But you love him or her. You conclude that you just can't help yourself and can't bear to face things alone.

And yet love was supposed to dissolve all your problems. Indeed, ultimately it can. But to happily love another, you have to also love and respect yourself. One-way love is really no-way love. Only doormats have the endless generosity required to sustain a one-way relationship.

So you more than lament fate when your relationship ends. You fear that now you'll be forced to go it alone. And alone means you're just you, and so you're less than complete. How can you go it alone if you're only half good? Feeling that way, even if a new growth opportunity presents itself, you may not really be able to explore it. Because you're trapped in the feeling that you've run out of time, run out of options. You're inadequate, so you panic.

Logically, this attitude is bad for the business of your recovery. If a business keeps making the same mistakes, they soon wind up filing for bankruptcy. If you keep making the same mistake that prevents your full recovery, your prospects for happiness could be kept bankrupt as well.

Why do people panic this way? Why does getting over a lover seem to inhibit our cortical functions? Why do people do the same self-destructive things over and over again? Some reductionists will tell you that it's just human nature, that we just need lots and lots of healing time from the pain that the loss of an intimate relationship causes.

But often it's not the wounds that the loss of a lover inflicts on you but your own long-standing sense of inadequacy that cries out for support. So in truth, it's likely that your own long-standing psychic wound just reawakened when you were in the middle to late stages of your failing relationship. It's the same wound that still hurts so much now that you find you're alone. Perhaps you hardly felt any pain at all when you were with your ex-lover. So just as it's natural to avoid pain and seek pleasure, you may have stayed in your relationship even after you realized that the basis for the relationship was more pain-numbing than loving.

So what do you do for relief? What will release you from panic, all on your own and without anyone outside to fill in your gaps? One of the simplest ways is to remember how you've felt in the past when the weight of fear and loss were suddenly lifted off your shoulders. Remember that you indeed have plenty of space and time, perhaps more now than before. Remember that you're not being measured and that all of your thoughts are your own.

When the desire to just hide from pain overcame your need to love and be loved, the result was an unbalanced relationship. Anesthetic relationships are very bad for leading whole and fulfilling lives. Ultimately, the ether wears off and you have to face a few things, things that were never insurmountable but may well be uncomfortable nonetheless.

But when you face your own real issues, accept responsibility and learn from them, everything changes. As your confusion diminishes, desperation will begin to fade and you'll almost immediately begin to make better choices.

And that positive process can commence at any stage of your anguish. All you have to do is make a decision. You can decide to remember that your happiness is not really contingent on the approval or acceptance of anyone else. Now you can stop, take a deep breath and relax.

Did your breakup seem especially ugly and hurtful? You may be confused because it ended so badly, yet you feel that you were as kind and loving as possible. Do you wish you could just go back and make peace? If you had a selfish lover or an unbalanced relationship, the possibility of a clean breakup may never have existed. Your ex may not love you anymore, but he or she may still dominate your view of the world, right or wrong. There is a sense of helplessness when you feel that your emotional fate rests in the hands of another. So why give that power to anyone else?

The answer to this is to take charge of your life. No one has the power or the right to determine your happiness. Once you make this discovery, you'll no longer use empty relationships to fill your own interior void, because you're always going to find people you truly enjoy.

By allowing yourself to calm down and clear your heart, you in effect, clear your emotional vision. Do you see now why your ex was not the person that you first thought them to be? Do you now understand why you allowed yourself to think otherwise? If so, you can feel proud of your insight.

You can also be proud that you entered into a relationship at all. It takes courage to love others and you willingly took the chance. You have to risk something to gain love. Not even Lloyds of London sells insurance against love's disappointments. But you're wise enough to know that if you fail to take any chances in life, you stand to gain absolutely nothing.

Now that your relationship's over, you have all the time you need to explore your own inner fullness. That's where you'll find the peace that can dispel panic at once.

 **TIP** . . . **No Hard Feelings**

Part of your pain is probably bound up in anger. Again, it doesn't matter who walked out on whom. A failed relationship produces the pain of grieving, and one of the typical emotional steps along the path of grieving is rage.

People have choices about their anger. They can let it out, or they can hold it inside, because they fear getting "carried away" by "bad" feelings. After all, you may actually feel that you hate your ex. And haven't feelings of hatred come to be labeled a crime?

Many other feelings can be stirred up by anger that may not find an adequate outlet. Anxiety, depression, a feeling of your own worthlessness, bitchiness, meanness, vengefulness, victimization, emotional emptiness, and a number of other "dark," or "negative" feelings may well be products of repressed anger. All may be dealt with more directly and effectively once the rage that inspires them is called out and examined.

Is your anger, or rage, or hatred really dangerous to feel? Not unless you're unable to accept them maturely, without "acting out" some infantile fantasy of revenge or control. Stalkers, abusers, and others with anger management and impulse control problems ultimately make their own problems worse. Impulsive behavior may only give them more grounds to feel self-contempt. And that self-hatred can further generate more anger, in a viciously self-destructive cycle.

Step One: No More Denial

It's ironic. Your first step to get rid of the risks and erosions that the passions of rage can cause is to come face-to-face with your own anger.

Do you hate your ex? Or do you hate yourself for loving and losing the other? Or do you hate someone else who helped bring your relationship to an end?

Carefully identify your most negative feelings about each of these people as precisely as you can. How do you feel about your ex, yourself, and any others who played a part in your parting? How have these sentiments influenced your feelings about the opposite sex? About God?

You must be as honest and careful in your answers to these questions as you possibly can. Otherwise you'll risk sitting on a time bomb of passions that may explode at any time... hurting you more than anyone else in the process.

Step Two: Self-Analysis

Once you've surfaced any feelings of anger, rage and hatred to those who played a part in your parting, you're halfway to your goal. But to get even closer, you're going to need to do some more introspection. Because of the speed of your thought processes, you probably don't realize that you feel anger after passing through a whole series of other feelings first. Often, these are feelings you barely notice because they scare you so much. Simply put, we usually feel anger in a self-defensive reflex. That means that when we feel threatened, we feel vulnerability before we feel anger.

If we first stopped to think about why we feel threatened, the anger may not need to be triggered. Reason can take its place. Examine the nature of your current circumstances more carefully, and you may conclude that your feelings about yourself are at the root of your anger, rather than your ex-lover or any other third party.

Think about it this way: what negative message about you provoked you to feel rage? Was it something like "I feel I'm unlovable," or "I feel so stupid," or "I feel like a loser," or "I feel like a kid, without any power," or "I feel guilty that I let this happen," or "I feel that I can't trust my own judgment, let alone other people."

Each of these messages has the same root feeling. Each of these messages says you think less of yourself, that your own self-esteem has been wounded so badly that you've been aroused to a set of fighting emotions — anger, rage, or hatred — each of which gives a little piece of the action back to you, their creator. In the court of your own mind, you've been judged and found guilty of contempt.

Step Three: Self-Respect Recovery

Those feelings of lost self-esteem can be redeemed. Once evoked, your passions will cool, and will ultimately find constructive outlets, like sarcasm-free humor. In the interim, be sure you don't swallow anger in a self-destructive fashion. If necessary, do some private screaming or pounding on pillows. Release your anger in a way that can't come back to hurt you later. Talk about your rage with people you can trust to help you to restore your perspective.

Ideally, find people to talk to about your anger who can help you see the good side of your own nature, your appeal to others, your basic human worth. In choosing people to talk to, find those who are comfortable with feelings of rage, anger, and hatred, but who don't need to nurse these feelings in themselves in order to accept them in other people.

You need to recognize that your ultimate goal is to pass beyond any anger you feel like directing to your ex-lover, or toward all men or all women, or to anyone else you may blame for your break-up — and that includes God. Your highest degree of sanity and self-protection will be found in responsibly accepting your own role in bringing about the end of your relationship, forgiving yourself and your ex, and finally, in setting aside or even forgetting the pain of your wounds.

Anger can be a useful medicine to help drive you away from your dependency on your ex-lover. But like any medicine taken when no longer needed, it can prove to be a self-destructive and addictive emotion that destroys your ability to live in a balanced, life-enhancing manner.

Day 13 Creativity

Your Lucky Day

Congratulations. You've come through nearly two weeks since your breakup and you're still with us, still making progress. That's one way in which this, your thirteenth day of recovery, is your lucky day.

But your real good fortune today will be to discover the wellspring which will give your rate of recovery a special boost. This wellspring is simply your ability to create your own prescription for promoting your own happiness. Even if you have never given yourself credit before for being a creative person, start thinking of yourself that way now. Everyone uses creative faculties in solving the everyday problems of their lives. Once you realize that, you can start using your capability to find new and even more effective ways to move back toward happiness.

As we noted at the outset of this book, our method for promoting your recovery is to urge you to use a variety of techniques to reduce stress and take a series of actions that will help to prevent you from succumbing to depression. As we've also noted, our tips' list of recommended actions for accomplishing this are far from exhaustive. We've invited you to come up with your own ideas for doing this; today we're going to insist that you do so.

Don't worry; we'll help you to start. Here are thirteen non-tip-tips that may give you some ideas of your own to make yourself feel better. Before you start reading, grab a pencil and paper and start making note of your ideas, so you don't forget to act on them later.

1) Treat yourself as you would a baby. Wear flannel pajamas with built-in socks, and give yourself a big hug before going to sleep. Hum yourself to sleep with your favorite lullaby.

2) Update your address book with information on how to contact the new friends you've made, and count them at the end of each week. List all of the new things you've tried today on your calendar.

3) Imagine that your thin skin is toughening up. Your recovery from your present hurt will help prevent any future disappointments from hurting as badly.

4) Make new plans to improve your life for this whole year. Then make a pledge to yourself that you will modify those plans only as needed. Even a meandering amble down an uneven path is better than standing still.

5) Budget time for daily moments of sharing your warmth. These moments will invite the caring that you need in your life right now.

6) Refresh and regain a positive attitude. No one owes you emotional paybacks for relationships past. Many people are like generals who waste time endlessly analyzing the last war, instead of devising new tactics to triumph in the next. If you keep reminiscing

about a relationship that no longer exists, you'll never catch up with the present. Keep it up and someday your prospects for a new relationship will die from fear of commitment. The worst kind of romantic may be the "curable" one.

7) Pull a reverse: put yourself in the shoes of your lost lover. Use this new perspective to better understand (*not* empathize with) the true motives that led to your parting.

8) Stick out your lower lip as you look in the mirror and do a huge pout. Then laugh at your cry-baby face, the one that's behind all of your whining, throwing tantrums and sulking about feeling left out. Remember that you are an adult with responsibilities and must find a mature means to address your new challenges. This 'second-childhood' behavior is often a cry to be re-parented. Work to make peace with your history, not to replay it.

9) That which obsesses possesses. If you've caught yourself wondering if your ex is having too much fun without you, imagine them as already lost in the arms of another person. Then dismiss that image. It's not your concern and any such thoughts will only waste your time. All you need to know is that your ex is living a life of his or her own choice. If you really still love your ex, you should respect their choices, no matter how much they may hurt you at this time.

10) Untangle the truth so it no longer suits your own immediate needs. Accept the realities, deal with them, heal from them and move on. Scream, kick, keep a journal, join an ashram, swim with dolphins, yell at your dog, even take your inner child out for inner ice

cream. Do whatever it takes to get rid of the ghosts of the past. Have the courage to admit that you were once in love, no matter how awful that may seem now, and heal forward from there.

11) Get busy, productively. Many people attack their pain by just burying themselves in busy-ness. But that usually won't create useful new insights unless your busy-ness contributes to your personal growth.

12) Every time you lift a glass of water or whatever you drink, before you sip say a silent toast to yourself, and praise all of your virtues. See how long a toast you can devise. Two minutes is good, five is terrific.

13) Make up a prayer for your own speedy recovery. Prayer is actually a movement to hope, one of the most sustaining of all human sentiments. So if you ever pray, now make it part of your learning and growing. Back all of your prayers with actions that take you to a better place in your life.

Did any of these tips inspire your own ideas for accelerating your recovery? Did you disagree with any of these tips? Good! What would you change to make the tip work for you? See how easy it is to be creative? Just spot a problem and come up with a solution of your own. Now that you've got that figured out, this really is your lucky day.

Use that creative capacity on your anxieties, which probably come from fearing that you may not merit the love that you need. This feeling will cripple your healing until you dispose of it. So turn those groundless anxieties into challenges. You're strong enough now to rise to these challenges for the rest of your life.

Love involves passionately giving to *and* taking from others, not getting utterly lost in their glories. If there's going to be a next time for romantic love in your future, be nobody's martyr. And if you must be a hero, plan to be a hero just for yourself.

⚡TIP . . . Getting Outside Help

If you're like most of the readers of this book, you've already decided to improve your feelings about the changes in your life, all on your own. There is every evidence that your active determination to improve your outlook will succeed. But what should those of our readers do who feel that they need extra help, beyond the standardized kind that we offer here, no matter how helpful our counsel may be?

We'd suggest that you start by doing some homework. For example, you will find an interesting article on the potential benefits of a variety of methods for treating mental health problems at the following Website: *http://www.apa.org/journals/seligman.html* The article appeared in the *American Psychologist*, a publication of the American Psychological Association, in 1995. It summarizes the findings of one of the biggest surveys ever conducted on psychotherapy's effectiveness. Appropriately, the sponsor of the survey was the well-known non-profit product and service evaluation publication, *Consumers Reports*.

The Bottom Line

Our own review of the study's findings produced a somewhat different set of conclusions than those arrived at by the author. That may come as no surprise; as a Professor of Psychology at the University of Pennsylvania, the author of the article, Martin E.P. Seligman, seems to have a horse of his own in this race.

The authors of this book do not practice as psychotherapists, nor as teachers of the art. Perhaps that's why we were most impressed by two findings from the study. First, Alcoholics Anonymous and its famous "12 Step Method" produced much higher levels of self-assessed improvement than any other type of therapy. Mutual support groups, family medical doctors, and all types of psychotherapists all produced roughly comparable levels of improvements for the first six months of treatment. After that, therapists pulled ahead. But we must interject some rather large buts:

· These days, who has an insurer that will pay for more than six months of therapy? And who can afford to pay for it out-of-pocket?

· The study didn't address the fact that most family doctors probably didn't want to continue working with patients with mental health problems for more than six months at a time, for professional as well as financial reasons.

· And finally, the study failed to measure the degree of self-assessed improvement in the large group of respondents who chose to deal with their problems on their own, or just with the help of family, friends, and religious advisors. So we don't know if "do-it-yourself" mental health tactics might not be fully as effective as formal therapy or medical treatment.

· Interestingly, psychiatrists, psychologists, and social workers all were associated with about the same degree of improvement, while marriage counselors weren't quite as effective as the rest of the mental (and physical) health professionals. No one type of therapy proved to be more effective than any other.

In short, most people who sought help from a mental health professional did feel that they got better, much better, within a reasonable period of time. But because of the nature of this study, we have no way of knowing how much help the passage of time alone brings to the healing of a broken or anguished heart.

The Mutual Support Group

We've carefully considered the findings from this report and many others, including studies of clinical efficacy. We've also talked about the utility of psycho-therapy at length (and off the record) with other distin-guished psychotherapists and psychologists in private practice and on the faculties of leading universities. As a result, we'd encourage those of our readers who want to add a formal treatment method to help relieve their anguish to seek out an appropriate mutual support group, or MSG.

The reasons for our recommendation are several, but most of them boil down to cost-effectiveness. For addictive conditions, especially alcoholism, the Alco-holics Anonymous, MSG route is a time-tested path to a more effective solution for those who are committed to change their self-destructive behaviors. And the cost of this therapy is quite often just your free time.

Finding the right group to participate in is a

critical issue. For more information on MSGs, you can start your research at our Website, on the page we devote to listing links to national mutual support group Websites, as well as to crisis intervention centers online. Your local newspaper, hospital, or community health center may also have useful information that will help you to identify a group that shares your kind of issues.

One-On-One Therapy

You may just be too shy to muster the courage to try a MSG. Or you may be too financially comfortable to consider setting aside the privacy of your pains in order to make the uncomfortably open disclosures that will be called for in a MSG. For you, it may only be suitable to share your pains privately with a therapist. Or your emotional problems may be severe and persistent, or be produced by conditions which prescribed medications or even surgery can relieve. In those events, one-on-one treatment by a mental health professional or doctor may be your best answer.

Whatever path you may follow to find answers to your unique problems, we of course wish you well. We would also encourage you to continue to practice the exercises and reflections suggested in this book. After all, there's no such problem as enjoying too much mental health, or just plain feeling too good. Given your body's natural tendency to heal its wounds, it's all a matter of time.

Day 14 Temptation

Hung Up At Midpoint

Let's see now: feeling alone, bored and miserable versus being back in the company we miss. Which sounds better to you? The wrong answer may seem irresistible, especially on a cold, lonely night. If the circumstances of your parting might permit it, you may figure, What the hey! After all, what harm can one more "last" get-together with your ex-lover do? So you call…

The hard reality is, such lapses can set back your recovery for weeks. The odds are excellent that you'll find such calls or visits are time wasted on an old lesson you have no need to relearn. But perhaps the pull of old habits still has a primal power over you. One sweet word, one little crisis, any excuse and you take the chance that things may have changed. If you've been cruel or cold about your end of the breakup, you may even feel guilty and become more vulnerable to more "false start" renewals.

So how did you finally break yourself free? A self-destructive method is to distract yourself by taking up with a new lover in no time at all. One model we know always has her new flame answer her phone in order to give her old flame the message that his fire had gone out. That's tacky, and invites retribution.

Another potentially flawed method is to turn fire into ice. Just act as though your ex is dead. Don't call them or answer their calls. This may make sense as a way to cut off an ex who has begun to act in an irrational fashion. But for most, it's a cowardly technique that almost always leaves the door open for more contact. Silence is no way to communicate the fact of a breakup. Silence is words unspoken, closure unrealized.

So it's time for your two-week check-up. This check-up is about one item and one item alone. It's about telling the truth. No, not just telling the truth to your ex. It's also about telling the truth to yourself. Acknowledge the truth of why this relationship did not serve your own best interests. Keep notes on those reasons right by your phone, if you must.

If you know the truth and respect your right to recover, you'll agree with us that dwelling on your old "it's over" woes just gobbles up your valuable time. Once you do that, it becomes impossible for you to remain vulnerable to backsliding.

Love And Compassion

Have love for yourself and the truth of your needs. And if your ex has tried to act decently, show compassion. Make it clear that you want the best for them but that "best" is not going to include you in their picture. It's closure, and it's final. Ultimately truth and compassion will win out. And those phone-calls that may have led you back in will finally end. That's when good bye finally becomes real.

There are now so many people who need your love in many new ways. Your recent romantic experience blocked your path to those who now await you. If you stay open to the prospect that your future holds new and even more meaningful relationships, where your love will be needed in surprising and perhaps more essential ways, that's what will happen. Your beliefs will become you.

And along the way, trust your instinct for growth. Healing is an ever-increasing receptivity to hearing the awakening truths of your own inner voice. Listen to that voice, and use its counsel to test your new strength on overcoming any risks you encounter. You do have power and when you exercise it, it feels like fresh air is renewing your heart.

TIP . . . Use Humor; It Heals

This tip may at first seem to urge you to do the impossible. Nothing seems funny when you're suffering the pain of losing your loved one. But one of the best things you can do to recover your emotional balance is to rediscover your funny bone. You haven't gone blind to your sense of humor, you've just got your eyes tightly shut to it right now.

You can fix that. And you should, because humor heals. And it also acts to anesthetize pain.

But first, we have to point out that people experience humor from size small to size large. Small may give you a feeling of amusement. It may even bring a bit of a smile to your mouth and the edge of your eyes.

Size large humor provokes a more dramatic physical reaction: laughter. Trying on any size humor will help you to counter the effects of the negative emotions you're currently feeling. But a real fit of laughter will give you the greatest benefits of all.

Like what? How about health and well-being, for starters?

Doctor Talk

Ask a doctor about laughter and he may tell you about its biochemical benefits. It cuts off the flow of the neuroendocrine hormones that go with stress, like epinephrine, cortisol, dopac, and HGH. Laughter kicks your immune system into high gear. Your body's T-cells and B-cells start cranking out disease fighting antibodies, while disease-beating Gamma interferon and salivary immunoglobulin A production goes up. Laughter's heavy breathing causes your lymph to circulate more vigorously and the oxygen level in your blood to rise.

A bout of hysterical laughter can be as invigorating as a brisk aerobic workout. It certainly seems to benefit those whose lungs need a cleaning, such as people with pulmonary diseases. And when you calm down after a good laugh, your muscles will feel more relaxed, your blood pressure may fall, and the immune system benefits in your biochemistry may be measurable for up to twelve hours.

Humor and laughter have proven to have a remarkable capacity to relieve pain and promote healthful sleep, even for those who suffer diseases like cancer and arthritis. Those who laugh regularly have lower resting heart rates. Lower rates of gastrointestinal and cardiac disease are reported for those who laugh easily at a wide variety of kinds of humor. These jolly people are even better at resisting infectious diseases.

So What?

All of these benefits that flow from having a fit of uncontrollable laughter may seem cruelly out of reach to you right now. But they're not. There are ways you can find your way back to your sense of humor, but they call for a deliberate search.

Unless you really love them, we don't recommend watching corny old comedies or cartoons to bring yourself to laughter. Too many unhappy people report that they just don't seem funny enough to make them laugh. And because one source of humor is the unexpected, or an element of surprise, don't go back to a movie or a book you once found uproarious and expect to find it as funny again.

We suggest you start to recover your sense of humor by realizing what it really is. Humor is actually a higher form of consciousness. A researcher studying the effects of the deepest levels of hypnosis put forward this idea. After hypnotizing his very best subjects, he found that at the deepest levels of induction they experienced an elevated mystical state much like those reported by adepts of all faiths. If that Godlike ultimate state is likened to "10 on a 10 scale," the researcher also noted that at "3 on a 10 scale," his subjects would often break into laughter, as they became aware of what the researcher called "The Joke." These subjects had at that point become aware of the wonderfully cosmic absurdity of the human condition. They laughed as they saw that desires of their own egos were rooted in silliness.

A well-developed sense of silly is also a good thing.

Rebuilding Your Funny Bone

To begin your own recovery of a sense of humor, or even just a childlike sense of silly along the way, try going inward on a voyage of discovery. Meditate a bit on the meaning of humor, and how it relies on feelings like anxiety and surprise in order to bloom into laughter.

Become an actor for a bit, and practice the spectrum of mirth, from a smile, to a grin, to a snort or a giggle, then a chuckle, and on to a full throated laugh. How well can you fake it? Can you laugh at yourself if you fail to fake a laugh in a believable way?

Stay on the lookout for genuinely funny stuff. Find something or someone that will make you laugh. Think about yourself with humorous affection. What do you do that strikes you as funny? What do you do that other people think is funny? Do you agree with them? If not, why not? Can you see yourself through their eyes, and get an affectionate grin out of you? Few characteristics are as appealing to other people as those who have learned to laugh at themselves, kindly.

Start looking for funny right now. If it's too late to go see a comedy at the movies, go hunt up a grin on the Internet. A lot of Websites focus on jokes, and some are even amusing. Use a search engine to find and sample a few. Or call a friend who always makes you roar with laughter.

Go see a friend and ask them to tickle your feet. Wear a silly hat to the office, or find a novelty store and start playing harmless practical jokes on your coworkers. Buy a new CD by your favorite comedian. Hire a clown, and pretend it's your birthday. Get your cat to chase the moving spot you make on the floor with a laser pointer, or scratch the side of your dog's tummy until both of you smile at how silly his leg looks as it reflexively scratches at the empty air.

Occasions for laughter are always all around you. All you have to do is use your imagination to find them.

Day 15 Celebration

Hurrah For Me

What does having time to yourself mean to you? Does it scare you, make you nervous? If you have trouble enjoying solitude, then there's a side of you that you're missing. Do you still imagine that you can't enjoy your life without a significant other? Consider the paradoxical truth that if you do want a great new relationship some day, you have to learn to reach more than a comfort level on your own. You have to realize a sense of deep joy and laughter. Wholeness and self reliance will attract your best prospects.

If you fear being alone, is it because you think it might lead to permanent loneliness? That's how being by yourself becomes some sort of punishment. But in reality, your new-found solitude is the best opportunity you may have found yet to find some true inner contentment and clarity. And while you may see this period as mere downtime until the next love comes along, it may be your chance to create a real sense of inner security.

This is an important milestone. You've made it to the critical halfway point, and it's now time to celebrate. Don't just reward yourself for the progress you've made in the last two weeks. Anticipate the great future adventures that your encouraging self-talk is already bringing you.

And this is a test. This is *only* a test, of your new-found ability to remember how wonderful you really are. So celebrate your willingness to give your life the happiness you truly desire.

So on this day, make your plans. Create a week-end getaway, if you can, and make this the start of discovering new joys within and around you that you weren't previously willing to acknowledge.

 **. . . The Divorce Shower**

Isn't it ironic: we throw a shower for people who plan to leave their parents in order to get married, but ignore the often more acute needs of those who leave a lover or a spouse. Our culture's rationale for such neglect is that we reward successful courtships rather than failed relationships. But must the end of a relationship always be seen as a failure? Can't it also be celebrated as a hopeful commencement, which can lead to a change for the better?

Even if only one side feels that way, now?

If one side feels damaged by the relationship's end, those who share a friendship with both sides may be hard pressed to reward either party for leaving the other. But at the least, any friend can recognize that the party who moves out of the common domicile is often the one who takes the blame for abandonment of the relationship. Let's call that person "The Leaver."

To be The Leaver often requires a number of

admirable charactcristics: courage under fire, a willingness to accept risks, determination in the face of resistance, the strength of character necessary to accept popular disapproval, the resourcefulness to adapt to change, and many other praiseworthy characteristics.

To the abandoned party whom The Leaver has left behind, these same characteristics are often seen as heartless insensitivity, brutal callousness, or worse. The Leaver may escape being seen this way only if the other person who stays in the dwelling they once occupied together clearly accepts his or her share of the responsibility for their break-up.

It can all amount to some pretty ugly stuff, to be sure. But under any circumstances, friends and associates of The Leaver should take a look at the material circumstances of The Leaver. Are they living out of cardboard boxes in a fleabag apartment, and cooking using the single pot they have to their name? Perhaps the family car is still in the hands of the ex, and The Leaver commutes on a bike.

If *you* are The Leaver, or even The Left, and find yourself living in what feels like an impoverished state versus your lifestyle before the end of your relationship with your ex, perhaps you can take action to help fix things a bit. Ask your best friend to help throw you a "Breaking Up Shower."

What's that? It's simple, really. A "Divorce Shower" is a shower thrown for only one party to a former relationship. It's a party at which The Leaver or even The Left is given a consolation prize by all who attend. You can even see if you can register with the Wedding Bureaus of the local department stores, so people will know what you need.

The friend who sends out the invitation to this shower must be careful about choosing those who are to be invited to this affair. Obviously, you don't want to invite those who strongly side with the other party. But on the other hand, why neglect those who are currently just acquaintances or work associates rather than intimates? The shower should be an occasion for sharing warmth and camaraderie, in which The Leaver or The Left begins to feel that they aren't alone after all.

Make the invitation a bit on the humorous side, so that people will feel comfortable saying that "yes, I will come." After all, you don't want them to feel as though they will be attending a funeral for the end of the relationship. That would be like asking them to bring gifts to honor the dead.

Plan well, to keep things lively and upbeat, and to have some fun. The event should be a bit like a coming out party. It should offer you a welcome back to the chance to build a new community of friends and lovers for the rest of your life.

Day 16 Remember

Losers Keepers

If this is one of those days when you still feel blue, you may think that you need to forget these terrible feelings of loss as soon as you can. But you're wrong. Wrong, if for no other reason than that people who can't remember their past are doomed to repeat it.

These days are your Iron Age, in which great interior discoveries and constructions will restore your ability to once again rule your kingdom. So don't let your constructions grow rusty. Don't let your own Iron Age become like the first, prehistoric one, unrecorded for posterity. Write everything down; keep a journal or diary. Your writings could prove to inspire the rest of your life.

If all of this sounds too much like schoolwork, perhaps you're one of those people for whom composing a sentence on paper is a pain in the… well, you know. But don't let this kind of an attitude prevent you from writing, even if you do it in your own private code. The more you write, the greater will be your odds of making a speedy recovery.

What's our proof for that promise? Think of it this way: your pain could be worse. You could be dying of cancer. And if you were, some good doctors would prescribe keeping a journal.

Margie Davis, an instructor at the Dana-Farber Cancer Institute in Boston, teaches a course called "Writing About Cancer." "It's worked for me and my students over the past seven years," Davis says, "…this kind of writing, reflecting back on how events have changed their outlook on life, is a way of releasing pent-up feelings that may not come out via talking or in support groups. When you write you have the chance to be with yourself and you'd be surprised what comes out through the pen."

Davis bases her work on research conducted by University of Texas psychology Professor James W. Pennebaker. Pennebaker's research revealed that writing down their thoughts and feelings about the source of their stresses helps people to heal on both emotional and physical planes.

Where should you start when you begin keeping your journal? Wherever you like. If you don't want to arrange it in the style of a diary, why not start by making a list that answers the following questions: "If I could send my ex to see a psychotherapist, what would I want to have fixed? What things did he or she do that hurt me the most?"

Your answers to these questions should be all you need to understand and remember why your ex is now part of your past. And to see the kind of person you want to avoid the next time you reach out for love.

So take solace in your discomfort. This may be your last opportunity to make careful notes on one of the most important growth experiences in your personal history. Your journal about these Days of Iron will add to your strength and give you memories you can take pride in when you reach more comfortable shores.

 **TIP** . . . **Breath School**

Did anyone ever teach you how to breathe? Of course not, you may say, everyone knows how to breathe. Life begins with an inhale, ends with an exhale, and what more do you need to know?

To relieve yourself of the stresses and anxiety you face right now, YOU need to know a lot more about breathing. The sum and substance of your insight into breath control probably amounts to no more than taking ten deep breaths when you need to calm down. Consider the fact that those who have made a careful study of the relationship of breathing to mental and physical health have developed hundreds of different breathing patterns which they use for specific purposes.

More than just yoga masters are interested in the uses of breathing control. A thoroughly Westernized "body-centered" psychotherapy system called "Rebirthing Breathwork" was developed 22 years ago by Leonard Orr and Sondra Ray. Its many practitioners now teach breathing techniques to "help activate and release stored stress, pain, and emotional trauma of all degrees..."

Interest in breathing techniques has even touched the medical community, since it now appears that breathing does more than simply supply the oxygen you need for metabolism. The breathing motions of the lungs, diaphragm, thorax and rib cage apparently aid the immune system by pumping lymph through your body. This system has even been called a "lymph heart." Further, the manner of breathing seems to act directly on the autonomic nervous system, with relaxed and full volume breathing serving to restore balance.

The Breath Test

Ask yourself: Do you find yourself sighing regularly or often? Do you wale up tired and stay that way throughout the day? How often do you have the sense that you need to catch your breath, that you are out of breath when you haven't been exerting a vigorous effort?

Experts say that you should be breathing about four to seven times a minute. They also say that while our lungs will hold up to two gallons of air, most of us take in only two pints per breath, and that's not enough. Most people breathe eight to fourteen times a minute, which is a sign that their breathing is too shallow to serve their bodies' needs. They often have failed to breathe naturally, from deep in their abdomens, allowing their bellies to rise and fall, effortlessly pumping their diaphragms with each breath.

If you are among these shallow personalities, spend a few minutes a day rehearsing a new way to breathe for the rest of your life.

Breathing School

Whether you like him or not, Tony Robbins is an inarguably successful motivational speaker. One of Robbin's most effective ideas is to spend 15 minutes each day practicing deep breathing. Robbins' claim that this will give you access to enormous reserves of vital energy have been tested and proven by thousands of his adherents.

Robbins' favorite technique is what is called the "Three Part Breath." It's easy to do almost anywhere, sitting or standing. Start by taking a deep breath down into the pit of your abdomen. Breathe through your nose. Then breathe more, till you fill up your ribcage, and finally expand till you fill up your upper chest. Imagine that your body is like an empty glass that you are filling with air from the bottom up. When full, reverse the procedure, exhaling from the top down to the bottom. To get out the last of the air at the bottom, pull in the muscles of your abdomen.

Got it? Good. Do it again. And again and again, for fifteen minutes.

Should you get bored with this exercise, try what some call Bellows Breath, which is said to be a great way to relieve stress. You have to be seated to do it. And don't try it while driving. Sit up straight, and blow an imaginary bug out of your nose by sharply pulling in your abdomen. Then relax, and inhale naturally. Repeat this sharp nasal exhale 22 times, then take a deep breath and relax for a moment. Go through three complete cycles of these 22 exhalations to get the most relief.

One exercise practiced by the Rebirthers is called "Conscious Connected Breath." They claim it has "profound healing and transformational qualities" but suggest that novices use it sparingly until trained by a professional. Here's how it works: First, lie down for 15 minutes. Inhale fully into your chest through your open mouth, and immediately exhale through your mouth in a relaxed manner. Keep this continuous breathing up with pausing for a quarter of an hour.

A more complex yoga breathing method is claimed to enhance health and ease one's consciousness. To do it, hold your left nostril closed while you deeply inhale and slowly exhale. Change to your right nostril for your next breath, and continue breathing through alternate nostrils for a dozen or more cycles. Repeat the exercise two to six times a day. This technique will also enhance your ability to meditate.

The Air Diet

Finally, if you wish to lose weight while you learn healthier breathing, we can offer you another novel diet idea. It doesn't call for changing how much, when or even what you eat. It just calls for you to change how you breathe.

Start the cycle by inhaling sharply through your nose, while pulling the corners of your mouth out into a big smile. Keep your abdomen relaxed to take in as much air as possible. For step two, after you've filled up your lungs, hold your breath while you pull your lower abdomen in and up. You can even help with your hands. For step three, while still holding that breath, do a bump, tilting your pelvis in and up. Tighten up your butt as you do. Finally, exhale through your nose, blowing as though you were encountering resistance. Feel your diaphragm tighten up under your ribs.

Repeat this pattern for ten minutes a day. Did you ever hear of an easier diet?

Day 17 Hopefulness

Ghost Flusters

The capacity for hopefulness is part of the ability to accept change. Hope accepts that it's possible for passions to die or transmute over time. Hopefulness sees that though yesterday's dreams fell outside of the truth of today, tomorrow's adventures still beckon.

Hindsight helps us accept that people change, and that's just the way of the world. Now that you no longer have a hurtful love in your life, your hopes will help you to complete your breakup. That's because hopeless people tend to let go of contact with ex-lovers long before they let go of even hurtful memories of that lover's presence. The true unfortunates cling to fading ghosts of their lovers for the rest of their lives.

Think of yourself and your own ex. Is it as if they're still here, talking to you, reacting to your thoughts, in effect still controlling you? Don't let this go on. Make it stop. Why keep haunting memories in your life? No one forces you to do this. Now is the time to let these memories go and look forward with hope.

Hopefulness is useful for preparing your future. It helps you release any ghostly, ghastly residue of that individual from influencing your life in any way.

It's time to accept that you are in the throes of change. Stop punishing yourself! Stop wasting time bathing in the dirty water of anger or depression. Anger sent inward is destructive. It paralyzes growth. And anger and frustration addressed to a love lost is meaningless, since the object of your anger doesn't hear you, doesn't care.

Letting go of a relationship that no longer exists for you can become a great blessing. It's like watching a movie through its ending. It may have been a good movie. It may have been awful. But when it's over and the lights go up, you know quite clearly that it's time to stand up and move on.

Loss often forces people to address issues in their lives that they had postponed examining for as long as they could. So, loss can present you with an unavoidable opportunity for self-transformation, to stop sleeping in your movie seat and embrace this new opportunity to grow.

Sharing time in the right relationship can be a peaceful joy. But enjoying those times you spend on your own can also lead to a real serenity. The challenge is to not become dependent on others to fill every alone moment. You don't need to mislabel solitude as loneliness. Don't sacrifice the things you can enjoy, like yourself.

In our culture, real love coupled with real passion is not supposed to be a "hold-back" affair. That's part of what makes it so confusing when a committed relationship ends. But when they do, you have to ask yourself if you were truly and deeply committed, with all of your heart and soul. A relationship needs a pragmatic, rational side, but without a deep and abiding passion, you'll never really experience all that it can yield.

Maybe you and your ex did have such powerful feelings at one time. So of course, it's one of life's great disappointments when the flame goes out in your last act together, and the lights go up in the theater.

If you use hindsight on your relationship, you'll see that there were times when you hit a crossroads of either committing more deeply or holding back. And eventually, if you held back, or if your partner held back, that may have been the moment the relationship faltered. And perhaps the mistake you made at the time was in not picking up the cue that it was time to let go.

But perhaps you were afraid. People often settle for less because they fear being alone. And if you ignored bad news just for fear of being alone, how could you then have expected to enjoy a real commitment — from yourself or from your significant other?

Real love accepts both self and one's lover. Hope opens doors, while romance evokes passion. If it fails to, it may have been a different, lesser kind of a love. Let the truth embrace you and don't be wounded by it. It's just trying to show you where you are. Show that you are truly growing by listening to the truths that speak to your heart. Learn to look forward to the joyous news that the future, and your foresight, will bring.

As soon as you can again look hopefully into your future because you are ready to be free, you'll then be able to move on. You may even decide to direct your life into creating a whole series of movies. If so, make your next one your best ever.

126

And don't get stuck hanging out in your lobby, hopelessly waiting for intermission to end.

 . . . The Meaning Of Suffering

While your recent loss caused you to feel pain, your suffering presents you with a chance to grow. Does that statement make you feel like you're tired of hearing people say "every cloud has a silver lining?"

If so, then imagine suffering a Holocaust. See yourself helplessly witnessing the deliberate destruction of all that you cherish. Imagine being thrown into the Nazi death camps and struggling to survive while those you love are taken elsewhere to be killed. Imagine then struggling against all odds to simply survive.

Out of such an unimaginable horror came a great book: Viktor E. Frankl's "Man's Search for Meaning." In this work, Frankl combines the original insights of a gifted psychiatrist with the inspired observations of a wise philosopher. This survivor of Auschwitz is known as the developer of "logotherapy," a system for psychic healing that stresses the primary importance of meaning in human life.

Essentially, Frankl teaches that life challenges us to discover the meaning of our unique existences. The meaning of one's life changes with time, but must always be sought. We are responsible for answering for our life's meaning. Meaning, Frankl says, derives from three things: from accomplishing a task, or from experiencing a value such as truth, beauty, goodness, or love, and... from suffering. Happily, unlike Freud, Frankl does not regard falling in love as a side effect of one's sex drive, but as something equally primary or perhaps even more basic.

The Meaning Of Suffering

Frankl tells the story of a doctor who had lost his wife. The doctor came to see Frankl for relief from the suffering caused by his wife's death. Instead of offering useless condolences, Frankl reframed the situation by asking the doctor what would have happened if the doctor had died and his wife had survived.

The doctor replied that this would have been terrible, that his wife would have suffered just as he had. Frankl replied that the way things actually worked out had spared the doctor's wife such pain, but with the price that the doctor now had to survive and mourn her. Frankl says that this answer satisfied the man, that suffering ceases to be suffering at the moment that it finds a meaning.

Frankl had helped the doctor to discover the meaning of sacrifice. As soon as the doctor had endowed his suffering with meaning, it changed his attitude to his fate. Frankl stresses that our main purpose in life is not to gain pleasure or to avoid pain, but to discover the fundamental meanings behind the things we experience.

While suffering isn't something necessary to find meaning, meaning is still discoverable whether we suffer or not. Unnecessary suffering should be avoided, of course, but should not cause anyone to feel shame when it proves impossible to avoid.

Discovering Meaning

As you experience the pain of your loss of a

lover, use it to empower your own voyage of discovery. What was the real meaning of your relationship, of its end, and of your responsibility for the suffering you now experience? If these meanings are not immediately clear, try asking the questions in a different way: if your relationship had not ended, what would that mean? What values did you experience in your relationship that you now miss the most? What values did you miss in your relationship that led to its end?

What positive values can you now list that will result from the end of your relationship? For example, will your situation force you to become more self-reliant, a better cook, or just a more self-responsible and autonomous person?

If you make any of these gains, then you must see that things could be worse for you, not *despite* your suffering, but *because* of it.

Making A Date With Happiness

When was the last time, you looked in a mirror and said, " I'm getting more wrinkles," "my hair looks awful," or "I just don't like the way I look." When was the last time you looked in a mirror and only saw your faults?

For most people, the correct answer is "this morning," or "in the last couple of hours." When was the last time you looked in the mirror and paid yourself a compliment? Too long ago to remember? Never? Look at it this way: if your mirrors had souls of their own and cared about insults, all of their spirits, hearts and faces would be irreparably broken.

Actually something worse occurs. We're all sensitive to the hundreds of media messages we receive each day. But you probably forget that one of the most impactful messages comes from your mirror in the morning. If you choose to, it will reflect back the worst side of you. Just tell it terrible things and then you'll carry those messages with you all day long. Could it be that after all's said and done, the worst verbal abuse you receive every day comes straight from your very own self?

So if you begin each morning and end each day

by paying a compliment or addressing some inspiration to that image in the mirror, you might be able to find more worth in yourself and the world all around you.

Being in a challenging but mutually committed love relationship is of course preferable to being party to a co-dependency in denial or in the narrow comfort of complacency. So now, after the fact of such a failure, you need to ask yourself what reflection are you now bringing to your life? If you're saying bad things to that mirror and then hoping that someone else's words will counterbalance those negative messages, then your relationships will always struggle to survive, with little hope of finding a truly healthy balance of give and take.

A healthy relationship requires both parties to make positive contributions to its vitality. The more interesting you make your own life, the less you'll have to depend upon others to do it for you. And if you can learn to enjoy yourself *by* yourself, your attractiveness to others will grow stronger. Be honest: do you want to build a relationship with electric connections, or just another shoulder to whine on?

Too many silly love songs insist that aloneness is next door to deadliness. But everyone needs some alone time. You need it if for no other reason than to once again reflect well and deeply on the meanings of your life. For example, think of the most important thing you expected from your ex. Was it reassurance? Do you still need that approval from another person, or can you supply yourself enough self-approval to satisfy your needs?

Actions based on jealousy or unbridled anger are really self-destructive options. They may seem to make living through lost loving easier than it might otherwise be under your present circumstances. But life is too short to commit yourself to reducing the fun anyone else may be having. You've had your share of whatever fun your ex-mate had to offer you. Now it's time for you to create your own joy.

Many couples who are play acting a lie need to falsely yet incessantly reassure each other of their feelings of love. If you're now ready to reject such behavior, you probably see that to get real love you need to give it freely in everything that you do. If you must ask another to give your love back, you'll soon become a burden and suffer rejection.

The best way to begin any relationship is as a "real-lationship." Don't fall in love with illusions or your own expectation. There's absolutely no point in entering into a relationship by raising your odds of fooling yourself. Every love is at its best when it's real.

So start now: get real with yourself. Looking inward, find the joy in yourself. Once you've found the way to that place, you can easily lead others to share it with you at any time you may wish to do so.

Enjoy your life; start today. Don't postpone finding joy to a tomorrow that otherwise may never arrive. After your passing, even if others remember you as a noble, self-sacrificing sort, you won't be around to relish your martyrdom.

So find your joy… now.

TIP . . . **Being Of Sound Mind**

Think about the sound of silence. Does it scare

you a bit? Silence can frighten anyone who hears the absence of noise as the sound of being... alone. Then, silence sounds like loneliness.

Yet we must accept the likelihood that for millions of years, mankind evolved in near silence. Take the measure of the sound of a gentle wind on an open plain. That's the diet which most often nourished the development of the human ear. Spiced up on rare occasions by the crash of thunder or the roar of an animal.

There are tribal peoples who still live among such simple silences today. Most of their elders retain the ability to hear a whisper across the length of a football field. While most Americans of the same ages have suffered mild to severe hearing losses.

What causes this difference? Abuse to our ears. It's why we associate silence with loneliness: we grow up with noise, and even accept it when the volumes are abusive, so loud that they cause us to lose our good sense — our hearing.

The signals of stress induced by noise begin to be evident in rising blood pressure when we are exposed to surprisingly familiar sound sources. Vacuum cleaners, airplane rides, lawn mowers and blowers without a doubt are stressors. And even riding the freeway in a car with the windows down can exceed the sound pressure levels where your body begins to show stress. Even with the radio turned off.

A Sound Diet Plan

What does all of this mean? It means you may be in a bit of a bind. You may need to put yourself on a sound level diet, to reduce the feeling that you can't deal with all of the things that are making you feel more pressure than you can cope with easily. If your job, or young children in the household, or even just the habits of a lifetime are exposing you to a source of sound stress, it's time that you faced the fact that you may have a problem. If you agree that you may, then we can help you to solve it. Here's what to do.

1. Learn to enjoy silence. For example, if you're in the habit of coming home and immediately turning on the TV set or radio, just to "have the sound of company," try putting off turning on the squawk box. That's especially true if you're a bit of a TV news addict. These programs thrive on scaring their audiences. Why take on the stress if you don't enjoy it?

2. Listen to small sounds with joyfulness. The rush of a wind, as it whispers through trees. Do song birds sing in your area? Can you hear children playing in the distance? Can you hear the sound of far away trains? Even the sounds of the highway you can't avoid hearing: listen to the rush — where are they all going?

3. Look for ways to reduce the volume of sound in your life. Throw away those headphones for your Walkman, for example. The devices should be banned as dangerous to your hearing if you're in the habit of cranking them up to loudly. Travel with your car windows up, and radio off. If you ride public transit, try earplugs or muffs. You'll be surprised to find that when you take them out, your hearing will seem to be better for a little while, too. Just a bonus.

4. Noise proof your house. Seal cracks in your doorways and windows, use heavier carpets and

drapes, soundproof the kids' room, things like that.

5.   Avoid yelling, whether in an argument or a crying spell, or just at a sporting event. The volume levels screaming can generate in your head can be higher than being close to a jet engine getting ready for takeoff. It's extremely hard on your ears and your throat, as well as stressing your heart and other organs.

In the periods when you really have an appetite for sound, listen to music through not-so-loudspeakers. Make your musical selections from uplifting or upbeat compositions that will raise your spirits without stressing your ears. Pay careful attention to the music you select, too. That way you won't have to turn it up so loudly that it won't help you to relax and regain your positive composure.

Day 19 Realities

Ex-orcise

One conclusion that will help move you forward is to face the fact that your ex was not The One. Not even close. Perhaps your parents or friends told you that this was The One. Perhaps your fantasies declared that this was The One and even your palm reader agreed. And of course, who wants to wind up being alone…

But what do outsiders know about intimate relationships? Some traditionalist authorities are almost militant in insisting that hope mixed with willingness can make any relationship endurable, and that love can work miracles. Well, that's true. And love can even alter chemistry and render tasteful prospects that may have at first seemed not to be your cup of tea.

But chemical reactions must be born from combining two substances, not just by setting them next to each other. You really can bring miracles to your life. But your love alone cannot revive a dead relationship. Stay at such a task for too long and you'll only wind up hurting yourself.

Many of the pre-boomer generation will disagree with this view, citing their own enduring relationships to prove that constancy conquers all. You'll often hear them talk about how hard *one* of them worked to make their marriage work. Their singular dedication was apparently unshakable.

Have times really changed? Those singular commitments to lonely but long-standing marriages may have once sounded admirable. But everything evolves, including equanimity and reciprocity in love. And if only one party winds up doing all the emotional work needed to maintain a relationship, that party is going to be over sooner or later. No couple could ever make such an uneven love miracle work in a way that permits both people to keep their self-respect. Today, everyone knows to demand better from love.

Let's look through the other end of the telescope. Were you your ex's ideal partner? If you were to describe such an individual, what would they be like? Does this description match you? If not, what does this teach you? If it teaches you nothing, perhaps its because (even though you're no longer wild about your ex at this point) you still sometimes miss some of the familiar comforts that grow up in every relationship.

That's the demon of self-defeating desires speaking to you with the voice of the past. There's truly one way to exorcise that demon, and to make it tell you the truth. The truth is that it's over, and The REAL One may actually be waiting for you in your future. And the truth is that you have better things to do now than anguish about having lost not *The One*, but *The Zero*.

TIP . . . Relaxation Prescription

Stress is your worst enemy. How can you calm yourself down when your world seems to be racing to

Hell in a handcart? Forget about illicit drugs. We strongly suggest that you try meditation instead.

This form of disciplined contemplation is not just a tool for mystical transportation. It's now an accepted tool of contemporary medicine. Ever since Harvard's Dr. Herbert Benson's best selling book *The Relaxation Response* was published in 1975, doctors have prescribed meditative techniques to relieve such symptoms as sleeplessness, high blood pressure, anxiety and panic attacks, and other stress-related afflictions.

Any number of religious traditions, including Christianity and Judaism, have evolved their own meditative systems. The universal idea behind these practices is that the Voice Of God can be heard by anyone who finds the right spot on their mental radio dial at which to listen to The Station.

That's hard for most of us, because our minds are so accustomed to being busy. As the Buddhists put it, our consciousness is like a monkey, forever chattering. Most systems of meditation therefore call for ignoring the monkey's chatter for long enough that he gets bored and shuts up. That's when you can begin to tune your mental radio to more interesting material.

Meditative Methods: The Basics

It takes many meditators years of practice before they begin to reach more elevated states of consciousness. It doesn't matter for our purposes here, however. We'd like you to explore the foothills of this territory rather than it's summits. So here's how to practice meditation for stress reduction in a way that will produce noticeable benefits within thirty days:

Set aside twenty minutes twice a day for meditation sessions. Use a place where you can be alone and undisturbed, at peace. Sit upright but in a relaxing, comfortable chair. Close your eyes, and (here's the hard part) let your mind go empty.

At first, your mind will drift back to thinking about things. Don't get upset when that happens. Just let a part of yourself watch those thoughts, and wait for them to drift away. To help yourself do so, you may wish to mentally repeat just one word or phrase (your "mantra"), or think about just one image (your "mandala"). Imagine yourself submerged under an ocean of air, and that your vagrant thoughts are like bubbles that float up and away from you, to the top of the sky.

For more information and ideas for meditative methods, we recommend the new edition of Lawrence Leshan's classic book, *How to Meditate : A Guide to Self-Discovery*. Amazon.com carries it for $8; twenty-seven years on the market, and it's still one of their 5,000 best sellers.

A Non-Meditative Method

If meditation is too frustrating for you, another technique that's often used to induce sleep or self-hypnosis may be a viable alternative. It's a great way to learn to put yourself completely at ease, that's sometimes called "progressive relaxation."

At least once a day, or whenever you feel "stressed out," find a place to be by yourself and lie down for about ten minutes. Focus your attention on your left foot as you count to fifteen. Pay attention to making all of the muscles in your left foot completely relaxed. Feel the tension leave your foot as you do so. Next, focus on your left calf, and relax all of its muscles for a fifteen count. Then your left thigh. Then your right foot, calf, thigh, all for fifteen counts.

Next, work your way up your trunk, to your arms and hands, and finally to your neck and face. Pay attention to the muscles in each body part, and spend a few seconds to carefully and deliberately make all of the muscles in that part of your body as relaxed as they can be.

Meditative Tech

Do you have access to a computer with a CD-ROM unit, sound card, modem and an Internet connection, plus a tape recorder and headphones? If so, good! You can now make your own brain-calming, self-hypnotic and/or meditative audio tape recordings. Just download an audio editing program called Cool Edit 2000 (CE 2000) from the Internet. It's current price is just $69.

Use your PC computer to record your own voice as you repeat a calming message of hopefulness. Then download Syntrillium Software's CE 2000 from *http://www.syntrillium.com*. CE 2000 is a simple and inexpensive little musical editing program. Install it and use it to mix your voice over a recording from one of your favorite music CD's of calming music. Now for the magic touch: process your recording through CE 2000 using its special brainwave-synchronizing recording process. What will that yield?

You'll wind up with a recording that you should

transfer to tape so you can listen to it through head-phones whenever you want. You'll have a recording that will encourage your brain waves to beat at a frequency of your own selection. Tune to Delta waves for sleep, Theta waves for mystical meditative states, or whatever you want.

Computers: gotta love 'em. When they behave without demons, that is…

Day 20 Exchanges

Ex-Rated

In an unhealthy relationship, a host of small affronts can collect over time to tear out the roots of a love. These events are not necessarily legible in what either party says, or does, or even doesn't do. They're in the nuances – savage little ambushes that strike when folks least expect them.

Those terrible nuances are always subtle. They're often very clever. And because they generally flew in well below your defensive screens, you didn't know why they hurt, you only knew that they did. So to the uninvolved eye, your attacker appeared innocent and you were made to feel foolish.

When people's feelings are hurt, when you feel victimized in some fashion, it's only natural to tell others about it and then try to gain support and resolve the cause of your pain. But in a troubled romantic relationship, in what you had once called "love," all bets are off. When hurting becomes chronic it's easy to get in the habit of trying to hold others responsible for your own failings. Or, the bonds that once held you can become ever more tangled because you too greatly needed the praise from a lover, and so became dependent on what they had to say. And as those once loving words were artfully twisted, the ground around the roots of your relationship gradually eroded.

In sum, that person who was supposed to lift you up kept you dangling, or worse, put you down. That was enough to convince you that you're a fairly inadequate lover. Now you scramble your way over the face of the planet, feeling a cloud of scorn following wherever you go. And whenever you meet new people, apply for new jobs, or see old friends, you're really not feeling like you're completely there. In fact, you're not; you're diminished. Why? Because your ex more or less told you that you… are… less, and so, that's… just… that.

As of this day, you must declare that you are no longer ex-rated. You no longer need any approval from someone who isn't even in your life any more. Why let their ghosts judge you? Why let *anyone* judge you? The only approval you truly need is your own. So start peeling away those other people's labels and get to know the you underneath all over again.

You can help yourself do so by briefly describing the one thing your ex often did to you that made you think less of yourself: Do you still have this kind of experience with any other people, friends, or co-workers? If so, write down three of the negative things you do when these kinds of experiences make you feel bad about yourself.

Do you understand *why* you feel bad? Write that down, too. What do you think *really* keeps you from feeling good about yourself? Are you willing to do whatever it takes to get rid of these negative feelings? All that you may need to do is change your perspective.

For example, try wishing for what you most fear...

TIP ... In Praise Of Paradox

"Say one thing, do another." Most of us say that about the way other people behave. Sometimes, we even recognize that we do it ourselves. We humans are by our nature self-contradicting creatures.

Viktor Frankl, father of Logotherapy, which is the psychology of meaning (see Tip #16), carries this insight two steps further. As a "wish is father to the thought," notes Frankl, so "fear is mother of the event." Said another way, it is a paradox of our behavior that what we most *fear* we will do, we too often *WILL* do despite ourselves. Walk into a crowded room being afraid of blushing or stammering, and we're almost certain to light up like a stuttering beet.

Classes Of Fear

Frankl teaches that fear can be realistic and thus immune to release by his therapy of meaning (as an example, the fear of death). Or it can be neurotic, in which case he suggests a wonderful trick of emotional jiu-jitsu, which he calls Paradoxical Intent. Form an excessively forceful intention to act in a certain way, and you can be almost certain you will fail.

For example, a man determines to be potent or a woman to have an orgasm. His very determination so preoccupies him with himself that he fails to pay attention to his own and his partner's pleasure. And this completely prevents him from forcing his wish to come true.

Sample Exercises

Are you irrationally afraid you will never get over your lover? Then try making any of the following wishes and then see if you can force them to come true:

1. Are you worried that your ex always seems to be on your mind? Then wish that a full day goes by without your thinking only about him or her. Urge your mind to think nothing about the good times or the bad, or the things that you most miss about them, whatever seems to be the typical thoughts that have preoccupied your attention in the past. After how many minutes do you discover that your mind insists on wandering to more interesting topics?

2. Are you worried about how much you're crying about your loss and your loneliness? Then make up your mind to cry for a full hour, or a full day, whatever will set the record for your personal best cry. See how long it takes before your crying jag dies a natural death (see tip #2).

3. Do you find yourself talking about your ex, or your loss, to excess? Are your friends getting turned off with listening to your grieving, or to your complaints? Get yourself a tape recorder, and lots of blank tapes, and make up your mind to record the history of your relationship with your ex, detailing every last inch of your grievances and your pain. See how many hours or minutes it takes before you find that you just don't have the energy any more for such a fruitless exercise.

Whatever your problem, make up your mind to do it to an extreme degree until you begin to gain some further insight into its meaning to you. Ultimately what

The Good Bye Book

will redeem you, bring you back to your common senses, is your sense of humor. All of these exercises will ultimately make you realize the absurdity of your irrational fears.

Day 21 Surrender

Unlocking An Armored Heart

Many hurt people are afraid to ever love again. They just want to recover from their last love and crawl off the field. Still others think they're fully recovered and that they simply made a bad choice in lovers or lifestyles. But even for them, breaking up may have been so hurtful, so humiliating that they simply give up and resolve to be content on their own.

Some people will feel truly relieved to be back on their own. But that's not likely to be you. Otherwise, you probably wouldn't have purchased this book. You probably feel most meaningful when you're sharing your love.

But right now, that's got to seem like an awesome prospect. What if you begin to fall again, only to be rejected? Or worse, what if this would mean that you'd been rejected once more?

This is the day for you to reject your capacity for cowardice. Cast off fear and begin to replace it with an appropriate hopefulness. Now, if anything's easier said than done, it's to offer dumb encouragement like "just trade your fear for hopefulness." Who wants to be afraid, you say? But in fact people often use fears to protect themselves. Fear keeps people from accepting invitations to risks. So oddly, a little fear can help us to feel relatively safe. But of course, our fears can also keep us from making any real progress on our path.

Even taken as a safety factor, fear can cause many unpleasant side effects, including boredom, loneliness, and unhappiness, to name just a few. While being alone's not a bad thing, alone-ness and loneliness are two different deals. We can be content on our own if we have a fair measure of love of ourselves as well as for others. But if you're no more secure about being alone than you are about being without love, lonely can be a very painful place to reside.

For many people, the best or even only way out is to find someone to love outside of themselves. You have lots of company if that's the way you feel you were made. "But stop!" you say, "what if I make the wrong choice and the hurt comes back all over again?" That apprehension alone shows why you must *not* manage your dealings with others primarily out of fear. Fear won't let you become whole.

Some relationship counselors will tell you that overcoming fear is a process that's going to take plenty of time. How much time? Not thirty days, they will say. Then, you might ask, how much time will it take, really? Thirty weeks? Thirty years?

We think that it's possible to overcome that fear in an instant. Do you have a moment? Because that's all you need to decide to make the right change in your attitude. Incidentally, we're not referring to falling in love again. That's truly likely to take you a matter of months, while you recharge your drained emotional batteries.

For this day, observe how many ways in which you've allowed your actions to be controlled by irrational fears instead of a promising hopefulness. How has fear caused you to make foolish and self-limiting choices? Or has it prevented you from making any decisions at all? Are the better options life has to offer rushing by you because your fears are too tenacious, too much of a habit of mind?

You don't really need those fears anymore. Now you can surrender them to some uncommon sense. By the end of today, make a list of the ways you'll put more faith in your hope.

 ## TIP . . . Good News For Your Nose

There's one sense that has an inside track to your emotions: your sense of smell. Your nose's sense of odors is directly wired into your limbic system, the old mammalian formation at the base of your brain where sensation and cognition are wedded to emotion to form what we experience in our conscious minds.

What all of this means is that there's nothing like a scent to bring back emotionally charged memories. It also means that your sense of smell can also create positive emotions to offset your feeling of being blue.

The use of smell to buck up your spirits is now touted as a New Age healing art called aromatherapy. We have found aromatherapy ideas useful for dealing with the blues, and even depression. Most often, aromatherapists will recommend specific fragrant oils from plants, called essential oils, as the client's conditions may indicate.

These oils are not taken internally, but are made a part of the air you breathe. The oils can be evaporated by heat from candles or by putting a drop on a hot light bulb. Or they can be more intensely dispersed if they have been infused into a burning stick of incense. You can also make a sachet out of the petals and leaves of the plants that have the aromas that you want, to put in your pillow, pocket or purse.

Do It Yourself Aromatherapy

There are a number of essential oils that aromatherapists recommend for depression. Some give you energy, and some give you rest. To play it safe, avoid using large quantities of any single essential oil for more than a couple of consecutive weeks, and once again, don't take any oils internally. You can ingest some of the herbs from which they're made, however; for more recommendations, see our tips about food.

Here are your best bets for scents that can lift your spirits:

· Bergamot's fragrance (Citrus bergamia) is a bit reminiscent of Earl Grey tea. It's said to be very uplifting and energy-sustaining. It is toning to the nerves and is often used for anxiety attacks. While it can even be used to treat a variety of skin conditions, watch out: never use it on skin which you plan to expose to the sun. Bergamot can cause burns and permanent spots on your skin. On the plus side, it blends well with other oils, such as citrus and herbs, and for that reason is often included as an ingredient in perfumes. It also disperses readily when heated in a lamp.

· Also worth dispensing with a light bulb: Clary

Sage (Salvia sclarea). While its aroma is said to smooth out women's menstrual cycles and to help reduce PMS, don't use Clary Sage if you're pregnant. It's considered both a sedative and a joyful euphoriant. Because of this effect, it is known as an aphrodisiac. Keep some handy for panic attacks, even in a personal inhalant. It's also safe to use in your bath water.

· A scented oil from Southeast Asia which is prized for its calmative properties is Jasmine (Jasminum officinale, grandiflorum, or sambac). Pure jasmine oil is a very expensive rarity, but worth it. It's said to build a positive frame of mind, and ease anxiety. Some even call it inspirational. Perfumers suggest blending it with Patchouli or Bergamot oil for a perfume that can lift your spirits.

· Don't stop now: other antidepressant essential oils include Lemon, Lime, Tangerine, Mandarin, Dill, Peppermint, Spearmint, Attar of Rose, Sage, Clove, and Ylang Ylang.

· To induce sleep, stock your pillow with dried lavender, hops, lemon verbena, rosemary, and peppermint. Try Chamomile too; folk medicine practitioners say its scent keeps nightmares away. Fixative agents like orris root or gum benzoin can be used to make these plant parts' scents last longer.

Where To Buy, How To Use

To find some of these oils and the gear you'll need to disperse them into the air, look in the Yellow Pages in a large metropolitan area for "perfumer's raw materials and supplies" or "aromatherapy" or "oils, essential." You might also find a reasonable selection of oils at a good health food store.

Once you find a store, let your own nose be your guide. While it might be useful to talk to a knowledge-able aromatherapist about which agents might be best for your needs, pick those scents you find have a posi-tive effect on you and your feelings. Also, feel free to blend essential oils to come up with a unique fragrance that causes you special pleasure. And use these cre-ations in ways that give you even more pleasure: to scent a room when you're about to do something you enjoy, or to make a soak in a tub even more luxurious, or just to cover up the smell of your beloved but wet dog.

Any happy memories you can build into these scents will make them that much more valuable to your mood in the future. You can not only use these things to create your own mood-lifting tools, but increase their horsepower by endowing them with pleasant memories of their own.

Day 22 — Responsibility

Wounded Child Day

Too many people just submit passively to the trauma and pain of their separations from lovers, believing that there's nothing they can do for relief but endure. Too many are unwilling to ask the right question, which isn't "How can I make the pain go away?" but "How did I get these wounds in the first place?"

Often answers to this last question involve shadowy memories of parents and some fuzzy and perhaps even paralyzing fears. As a result of your attempts at self-analysis you may next get angry at your parents. But you may not be quite sure why you feel that way, or how your interactions with them resulted years later in the termination of a relationship with somebody else that you loved.

Conventional Wisdom ("CW" for short) asserts that whenever we go through a trauma, our internalized parents, living or dead, can clearly be heard whispering their counsel and judgments, whether we like it or not. Of course, as CW teaches, whether you're nineteen or ninety you may have a wounded inner child who stops you from attaining a well-deserved happiness. So in the spirit of this type of wisdom, let's call today your "Wounded Child Day."

Some people do require extensive therapy to deal with their childhood traumas and to achieve resolution and peace. We don't mean to suggest to those people that we have a better option to offer. It's just been our observation that some people waste too much time on coddling, or even spoiling their own inner children when their time could be better spent on learning how to gain entry to an adult's kind of happiness.

Maintaining a childlike openness and spontaneity can help you to foster your hope and optimism at all times. But poking open childhood wounds that may have already healed is a poor waste of time. It can also prove to be quite unfair if you wind up blaming others for damage that no longer really exists.

However, just as optimism can create happy outcomes, believing that your formative psychological wounds are still open will certainly go far to keeping them fresh. And these open wounds will someday make it almost impossible for you to establish a truly healthy intimacy. Instead, every relationship you enter will be an unhappy threesome: you, your loving partner, and your wounded child.

Children lack the means to resolve grown-up issues. But as adults, our rational faculties can often help us to make resolutions fairly easy to reach. Once again, this is of course not always true; those who have suffered severe traumas may need professional counseling. But for many, the best way to "carry on" is simply to see their past traumas quite clearly and then let them go.

For example, let's suppose you were a child who suffered severe abandonment pains. Now, whenever you break up with a lover, you experience an inordinate degree of anguish and heartache, far more than most people you know. Now, imagine you recall that the first time you felt this way was at age 10, when you were separated from your parents and sent to boarding school. So much later you seemed to relive the pain of that separation every time you went through a breakup. But now you've found the roots for your pain. Sometimes that knowledge can be enough to ease all of your relationship anxieties, and allow you to experience something more meaningful the next time around.

In the meantime, you needn't be as lonely. And you won't feel like avoiding or entering new intimacies for some very wrong reasons. Thus far, there's some truth in Conventional Wisdom.

But after this point, why let a hurt child whose problem's been solved still run your life? If the source of your problem's been dealt with, that makes no sense at all. If you can let your traumas go after some simple introspection, get down to business and do it right now. Start by describing the emotional state of your inner child: describe why that condition's holding you back. Was there a time or occurrence before which separation didn't hurt you as much? What happened?

Are you ready to forgive or at least understand the creators of your pain? Or do you still need to let this old wound fester and perhaps ruin your ability to form positive relationships as your future rolls by?

You're an adult now. Do you still think it's wise to let a child decide your affairs? It's really not necessary to let anyone do so; the following tip spells out more specifics on how to stand as an adult on your own.

☀**TIP** . . . **Your Emotional Flashlight**

Whenever you feel gloom coloring all of your other emotions, you can throw some light on large parts of the darkness. We'd like to help you conduct a rational self-analysis. Even though it calls for you to use reason to evaluate yourself, it still may be painful in part. If so, put off the hard questions until you're ready to answer. The objective of the exercise is to help you to discover the sources of your pain, so you can better understand your own emotional soft spots and needs.

For this emotional inventory to be useful, you must be honest with yourself at all times. If you're in the habit of being either too hard on yourself or indulgently self-absorbed, break these habits for a moment. You want to be as objectively fair in your answers to the questions we'll ask as you can possibly be.

Your Body Of Emotions

Your emotions have just taken one beating, due to the loss of a central love relationship.

Your recent loss is a fresh, open wound. But let's now look for scar tissue left by old wounds. It might even be helpful for you to take notes on what you find as you do this. Some of the discoveries you may make may have originated in painful experiences you actively wish to forget.

That desire to forget can come around to hurt you again, as it may cause you to overreact or even panic if you encounter similar circumstances once more. Why take such a risk?

Uncomfortable Questions

Let's look at your own estimate of yourself as a lover. And we don't mean sex partner, though that may be part of it. We want to know the strength of your love ego: Are you sincerely capable of feeling love for another person strongly? Are you capable of openly expressing your loving feelings in an attractive manner that invites a fair exchange?

If you must, admit it: are you afraid of expressing tender feelings? Do you encourage lovers to see you as a different person than who you really are? Do you perhaps feel less than fully lovable just as you are? Do you feel that lovers of the opposite sex are so powerful, they're dangerous, and mustn't be trusted with knowledge of how vulnerable love makes you feel? Do you actually have a prejudice against their sex, an attitude that prevents you from seeing the person you "love" as totally lovable, by their very nature?

Ancient History

Have you had a series of unfortunate experiences with intimate others? Are you "unlucky in love?" Trace it back: what is there about you that may make it so? Did your parents or other loved ones expose you as a child to failed relationships or a family history of divorce? Is this history part of your anxiety?

What are your other intimacy issues from your childhood? Don't just say "dysfunctional relationships," that's nothing but a catch phrase. What kind of love failures did those you love suffer? Addiction-based failures—sexual, alcohol, drugs—or other causes: money, abusiveness, or just loss of interest? Do you see any parallels in your own expired loves that reminds you of the failed relationships that caused you pain as a child? Do your fears—fears of abandonment, unworthiness, inferiority—spring from messages you picked up from your parents or peers as a child?

How many of the people who wounded you did things that you have never forgiven them for? How many of them can you now release with forgiveness for their failings? Especially when those failings are character flaws that you now recognize in yourself...

Closer To Home

Why did your most recently failed relationship die? Don't overcomplicate matters: explain why it failed due to your actions or inactions alone, and in one sentence or less. Then explain why it failed as you imagine your ex-lover would, in one sentence or less. What would you change now in hindsight that would have made for a happier outcome? Can you see this as a mistake on your part, something you can learn from so that you never have to make the same mistake again? What steps can you take to prevent yourself from making that same mistake again?

Why not start now?

See The Future

Like it or not, bygones are bygones. Looking to the future, what kind of relationship would be ideal for you? How do you go about building a relationship like that? What do you have to do to make it possible to find someone who will be able to play a part in your dream, and in all of the rest of your life?

Day 23 Pathways

Always A Way

Even as you pass through the most painful events, there's always paths to be found leading back to good times. Some of these paths may cause you to hesitate, but ultimately you have to decide to move on. Is there anything that could make your decision easier? Yes, absolutely. It can be found in the appeal of enlightenment. Not in our just droning on about "healing" and "process" but by offering you a sudden and immediately transforming enlightenment. Like a light going on in a very dark place.

Any day can be viewed as a good day if you've learned something new and important, really learned it. Because when that happens, when that new awareness becomes a genuine part of your emotional toolkit, that means there's one more bit of suffering that you'll never have to go through again.

Yesterday's exercises proved to be both exciting and difficult for others who've done them. If you've really been working through your old issues and are now taking bandages off wounds that have already healed, you're most of the way through a difficult task. But this is one of the best pathways to the better places to come.

If you can dream up an ideal romantic partner today, how different will the person that you see be from your ex? Is your new vision based upon the qualities of character and feeling that will produce a love that's really good for you? Or are your specifications just based on a new-found distaste for anything that might remind you of your ex?

If you're ready, really get into creating a carefully detailed vision of your potential new lover. Ask yourself:

• Why do you trust this person? With your loyalty? With money?

• Is this a person who keeps growing and learning?

• Can you see yourself with this person ten years from now?

• Which of your secrets can you share with this person?

• How much will this person need you for self-esteem?

• Will this be a person who will remain cool in a crisis?

• How judgmental and critical is this person of others?

• How will you feel after spending four hours alone with this person?

• What will this person have to do to make you feel happy, at peace, complete? Ski? Dance? Pray with you? Play with your cat? Talk dirty? Fix cars? Send flowers? Play chess? Cheer for your favorite teams? What kind of person could teach you new ways to be happy? How?

When the time is right, it will be as the song says, "love is everywhere." But too many people today are deeply embittered and hardened. These feelings have sentenced them to blockage from loving, let alone bliss. And that leads us to the most important question of all:

• Have you decided that you aren't here to love and be loved? Are you feeling so hurt, so full of anger and mistrust that you're willing to deprive yourself of what might someday prove to be some of the greatest times of your life? Do you wish to suppress your ability to share love with another?

Tough questions, but your answers need to be developed in the most careful of terms. Why? Because love in all of its flavors is the soul food of human existence, and you deserve your seat at the banquet. Love's nourishment can revitalize anyone who is able to fully digest it.

Love's not reducible to all of those sinks full of someone else's dirty dishes you've washed, or a bitter pill you've already swallowed. Here's your real enlightenment for the day, if you're ready to receive it: love is your essence, whether you've forgotten that or not. Just answering the questions listed above can show you how much you've grown stronger in your ability to again feel love, at least for yourself. And show you how far you've grown away from the "love" for your ex, which had probably deteriorated to nothing more than a hurtful dependency.

Learning means taking paths you've never followed before. Your discoveries along the way will refresh your spirit. And if you get discouraged at times, that's still okay. If you're serious about moving on in your life, all you have to do at this point is be willing to have your path be an enlightened one. Look upon love of all kinds as forming the paving stones for your shortest path to happiness.

 . . . Affection Protection

Picture your emotional life as an archery target. You are the bull's-eye, the circle at the center. The first ring that you placed immediately around you was the person you loved most, who is now gone. The next ring out from that is formed by your relationships with your friends and your family, people with whom you feel a sense of closeness. The next ring out consists of your associates and acquaintances, people who you either have just begun to know or to whom you don't feel any sense of closeness.

Break-ups create conflicts on any number of fronts. As the person nearest the center of your emotional life has been removed from your life, you will naturally look to the next ring for solace. You will turn to your friends and family to express your innermost feelings in a flood of self-disclosure.

Take Care Of Yourself

Such openness is not without risk. The odds of an unfortunate surprise happening to you may depend on how bad the results of your breakup are for others.

If you're just breaking up with someone with

whom you've had a mad fling for a month, you can usually expect your friends and family to be trustworthy and true. But the more your dealings with people you regard as your friends have become intertwined in social affairs that were shared with your ex, the more you need to carefully ask yourself where your friends real loyalties lie. It may sound paranoid, but a certain measure of care can help to protect you from finding yourself getting sandbagged by a "friend" or even a family member who proves to be a hostile witness when your divorce comes to court. Or whom you later discover to have had intimate relations with your ex before or after your breakup.

Impossible? Experienced family practice attorneys claim that the odds of such disappointments may be as high as 50%. Ask your divorce lawyer for counsel. Or ask your friends who've gone through major breakups themselves. Lots of relationships end with games that are played fast with a very hard ball.

Prescriptions

Oddly enough, it's often easier to disclose yourself honestly to a perfect stranger. If they judge you negatively, what have you lost? The positive regard of someone you don't know and may never meet again?

1. So our first rule is that if you have to let someone know about the reasons for the end of your relationship, don't put yourself at undue risk. Unload on a stranger, or a new acquaintance who gives you the sense they're willing to listen to your outburst without passing judgment.

2. Rule number two: don't discuss the details or

private issues behind your divorce with your minor children. It will only disturb them, and put them in a compromising and painful position of feeling you want them to choose between people they love. Don't drag children into quarrels or negotiations about their disposition. Mediation, arbitration, and settlements are strictly grown-ups' affairs.

3. Rule three: if you're involved in a divorce, take notes when you talk to your attorney. It's easy to forget some of the unpleasant counsel you'll get, unless you make sure you have a record for later review.

4. Rule four: if there are child custody issues involved, or if there is any prospect of property disputes in a divorce, use separate divorce attorneys. The profession does include some decent, caring people; screen your prospects with care. And remember that a court may throw out a divorce agreement that has been drafted by one lawyer who has worked for both parties, if either party later changes their mind. At that point, both parties must begin the process of negotiating a resolution from the beginning. It's an avoidable extra expense.

5. Rule five: keep at least the family pet if you can, and get all the love you can from it. People who love and keep pets have longer lives, for a reason. If you don't have room for a dog or a cat, visit a neighbor who owns one, and make their pet your friend too. Or at worst, visit your local animal shelter and see if you could serve as a volunteer there.

6. Rule six: as soon as the dust has settled, when you feel like your feet are back on the ground and you've finally negotiated any divorce agreement, hold a

party for those of your friends and family who have stood firmly by your side through it all. It's time to thank them for their commitment to you, and to confirm your readiness to move on with your life. As the saying goes today, it's time for closure.

$\mathcal{D}ay\ 24\ \mathcal{V}ision$

Choosing Happiness?

It was Alfred Lord Tennyson who said, "'Tis better to have loved and lost than to never have loved at all." Foolish dead poet, you say; how could it be better to have loved and lost?

Perhaps Tennyson concluded that even loves lost may eventually be remembered as hilariously comedic or marvelously tragic when one gets enough emotional distance away from the pain. Pain is not your punishment for having played the fool; it's just a wound that will heal. Will the wound leave a scar? Perhaps; look upon it as your badge of honor, an icon that shows that you're vitally alive, and willing to gamble on the glories of romance and intimacy.

"But," you may say, "why does it have to be me?" If you're still feeling far enough down, it may seem that most of your friends and relations never had to go through the kind of heartache you're now trapped by. Perhaps you think that for generations past, boy met girl, they fell in love, courted and got married, and that was that: easy.

And in fact, there may be some truth in that simplistic perception. Loving once offered most people fewer acceptable options. When there weren't all that many ways to find happiness, the choices were easier. The idea of staying single was often sneered at, in the way people used terms like "spinster," "bachelor," "old maid." It was a "one size fits all" prescription for living. Conform or be ostracized.

It's not Kansas anymore, Toto. You are now free to choose from a large menu of lifestyles. And never before have we had such long lives and fat wallets with which to savor so many rich dishes. We have more space, we have more time.

Or do you? You can try on different life- and love-styles but can you really cast free of the bedrock that supports your loving, your sense of mutual acceptance, enjoyment of constancy and fulfilling dedication?

In reality, the popularity of lifestyle swapping experiments crested in the Free-sexy Sixties and Seventies, to say nothing of the Roar of the Twenties. Such cycles of physical friskiness go back at least as far as Sodom and Gomorrah; hedonism is certainly nothing new. And the inevitable consequences are nothing new, either. The fact is that we cannot simply do anything we want with anyone we wish to, if for no other reason than because as ever, hearts can be broken.

So it seems that easy intimacies may pull people in too many directions. While the pursuit of happiness now goes faster than ever before, the absence of speed limits means that we may encounter more crack-ups than ever as well. You have to choose wisely. Bad choices used to just be a sad thing. Today more than ever they can spell your demise.

Even if you decide to spend the rest of your life alone, make sure your choice has been made for sound, positive reasons. Are you going to remain alone because you're truly happier that way, or have you gone into solitary confinement because you've convicted yourself of a failed romantic experience?

What good is living a longer and healthier life if you have to spend much of it in fear or embittered paralysis? All that extra time on your hands...

It's no good trying to cut your losses by spreading your bets, either. Some sufferers try jumping from one meaningless affair to another, hoping to keep from getting hurt by investing in no one. But just as healing is cumulative, so is hurting. And meaninglessness can hurt worst of all. If you're lucky, such experience teaches that you need to make better, harder choices. You need to 'interview' better, think more deeply and act less impulsively in response to your options. But you'll find it difficult to do that if you simply view being alone as a big, dark hole that must be filled as quickly as possible.

So it really is better to have loved and lost, if it effectively teaches you that you have the wit and confidence to say 'no' when you know you should. Then comes the question: "How do I know when to say NO?" You've already determined that enough was enough in that old, dead relationship. So it ended. Now, how soon are you going to stop feeling wounded and move ahead once again in a healthy and open way? That's what *real* freedom feels like.

It will take both graciousness and strength of purpose. Developing a powerful sense of purpose is a lot like going through a series of full body workouts. At first, you may ache and feel quite discouraged. But if you listen carefully and openly to the important new lessons that come your way, the worst loneliness you may ever experience after future encounters will prove to be brief and more readily endured.

♀TIP . . . Master Your Subconscious

One thing that those who grieve learn quickly is the unpredictability of their emotional roller coaster. The experience teaches that your subconscious mind seems to have a rhythm and an agenda of its own. But there are ways to successfully negotiate with your subconscious. One technique used to do this is called "creative visualization."

Sweet Dreams

Think of this technique as "wishcraft." You really can use it to persuade the deeper recesses of your mind to let you get what you want by visualizing the outcome you desire.

Professional athletes have proven the basic technique to be effective. Many of the most successful ones now include creative visualization in their training for major events. The way they use it is profoundly simple. They simply imagine themselves, in as much detail as they can muster in the eyes of their minds, doing exactly what they want to do, perfectly. Call it mental rehearsals, if you will. They repeat and repeat these flawless performances until the vision seems to play itself out, by rote.

It's believed that the very best time to conduct these flawless performances is in the very first moments of awakening, and during the last moments that precede going to sleep every night. It's at those times that the brain is often in what has been called a hypnopompic state, with the subconscious disarmed and ready for reprogramming.

What should you envision? How about yourself, free of grieving and once again at ease in a setting that gives you pleasure. See yourself as confident, once again unburdened, perhaps even with your "ready for romance" battery recharged and sending out all of the right signals.

Unlimited Affirmations

Another reality programming technology makes a different analysis of the operation of the mind's lower levels. This system regards your subconscious as a bit simple minded. It tends to believe whatever it hears, or sees. And if things don't match up, the subconscious will apparently do everything in its powers (which are apparently considerable) to make reality match what it's being told.

So here's what you do, according to this system:

1. Look into your heart, and describe in one short sentence what you want for yourself. Describe this desire in the present tense, *as though it has already happened*: "I'm so happy I've gotten over (old what's her/his name)."

2. Say this sentence out loud, so your subconscious self will hear it (this theory says that your subconscious mind listens to, and believes, everything that you hear). Say it three times every morning in the shower, or mutter it as you go to sleep at night.

3. Take a break at work, get relaxed, and write out your sentence three times on a piece of paper. But just to make sure your subconscious notices what you're up to, write the words as small as you can, without straining.

4. Do this for a week. By now, your reprogramming will have begun to take effect. So it's now time to look into your heart again. Have your feelings about your heart's desire changed? If so, reflect that change in your new affirmation for the week, and include it in all of your verbalizations and visualizations.

Over the course of your thirty day healing process, you should have had the opportunity to review and evolve your expressed desire three to four times. As your recovery progresses, watch as your ambitions for yourself increase in boldness and hopefulness. Some believe that there are only two rules which will limit what you can accomplish using these methods: you must believe, right down to your core, that you actually can and will attain what you desire, and second, that no one else will be harmed if your desire is attained.

Day 25 Rebirth

"New" Feelings

Remember the longing you used to feel for your ex? Perhaps it felt like a knot in your gut in the days immediately after you first broke up. Think of that feeling now, right at this very moment. Can you make yourself feel that same intense feeling of loss?

Come on, try hard, perhaps you can do it.

It's gone, isn't it? And that fact carries a very big lesson. The lesson is simple: the love you thought you had lost at that time, the romance that seemed so critical to your happiness, was perhaps delusory and was certainly dispensable. As we suggested at the beginning of this book, dropping your delusions can be almost as tough as kicking an addiction. And for many of you, it probably was. But if you made it this far, you now have more freedom to make the choices you truly want for your new future.

One dilemma you need to face is potential confusion about the many levels of what "new" really means. Some psychotherapists believe that people build all of their emotions out of nothing more complicated than various mixtures of pleasure and pain. They believe that by as early as age six, we will have created the full palette of colors for all of the emotions we experience for the rest of our lives. So, your key to feeling new peace may be found in relearning earlier, more innocent ways of experiencing your world. The ability to do so will help you to recover something wonderful about you and your nature.

There's one big reason for your success to date. It's your willingness to face the truth about how you really felt about yourself when you were with your ex. In going through this sometimes-disturbing process, you have gained a new freedom to share your love for yourself and for others in the ways that you really had always wanted to do so.

An important component for being able to love another in a truly healthy way is realized when you learn how to love who you really are. If you don't, perhaps you now see that you will connect with others for basically the wrong reasons. You'll depend on them for approval and self-assurance because you were unable to see the true beauty and innocence that is built into your nature. In short, you stopped employing more childlike, loving ways of experiencing yourself and your world and finding your own creative joy in it.

But you've already stopped banging your head against that wall. You don't need to do it again.

Your fresh combination of new and original feelings will provide you with a real personal rebirth. After you've thoroughly explored the bedrock of your emotions, you'll be ready to step up to a higher kind of experience. As long as you can really recover your sense of innocence, you will be dumbstruck with joyous wonder at the richness of pure feeling. And as a consequence, your view of the world will be vastly enriched and extended.

Look around you. Can you yet sense the fresh possibilities? Prepare yourself: old feelings may rush into your heart like a soft breath of magic. Feel the possibilities. All of these once again new, long forgotten feelings. And the more you're willing to embrace them, the more possibilities you'll have to create a richer, more rewarding new life.

Welcome home to that wonderful child you were hiding inside.

💡TIP . . . Grieving, God, and Giving

The end of your relationship has caused you pain. Naturally, you want your pain to stop. So you try ignoring it, putting it away, acting as though it doesn't trouble you.

Some people are better at this trick than others. Don't think of them as lucky. Think of them as human time bombs, ticking away with fast-rising internal pressures that their repressed feelings have inflamed.

Many of us live on a psychic knife-edge. If we can use our will power to stop acting self-destructively, that's good. But if we try to control the feelings that inspire those actions, it can lead to all kinds of problems. In more extreme cases we see obsessive-compulsive disorders. Some people who foster this illusory self-control wind up as addicts to sex or substances.

"Twelve Step" Redemptions

So you can't stop grieving your loss by just pushing it down. But how can you hope to deal with your pain? The many "Twelve Step" programs modeled on Alcoholics Anonymous have consistently adopted a method that seems to work for a high percentage of those who employ it.

Usually, these sufferers are not ready to adopt this method until they have "hit bottom." That is, they arrive at a final stage of despair which leads them to realize that they are helplessly unable to control their behavior, but desperate to find a solution to the problems they've caused themselves. At that point, those who turn to an organization like AA are told they must consistently acknowledge that they are powerless before their enemy (alcohol, sexual impulses, drugs, etc.). And then they must take the one step critical to effecting their cure.

They must put their fate in the hands of a Higher Power.

Atheists Welcome

None of these organizations demand that atheists or agnostics suddenly find faith, or worse yet attempt to simulate a religious awakening. They simply suggest that people like these look within themselves, and recognize that beyond their egos, their "I'm me" sense, all of them have an intuitive sense of a larger entity. Call it our Self, or simply Higher Power. Names matter less than the act of surrendering yourself to the assistance of this agency.

What does this suggest for you? If we follow a parallel form of logic, we could say that you are powerless before the enemy of your addiction to the memories of a person. Perhaps you have reached your own bottom, despairing at the pain the loss of this person in your life has caused. If so, try putting your care in the hands of your own Higher Power.

Where To Surrender

Do you need a place to effect your surrender to your own Higher Power? Why not do it in a house of worship? People of all denominations can find the peace and contemplative solitude they need to perform such an act by going to any church, chapel, synagogue or temple that leaves its doors open to the public when a service is not being conducted. Larger hospitals usually provide such a full-time facility, often featuring a non-denominational design. The spiritual aura of these places can help to focus the minds of those who need to give themselves up for a change.

If a house of worship isn't your scene, try giving yourself to others. You might start by spending a little time with a lonely young child. Their simple way of approaching life can refresh your sense of your own latent innocence and purity. Or offer your help to others who suffer: the homeless, the destitute, the physically afflicted. Serve as a volunteer. Don't be afraid of the pain of compassion.

By giving of yourself unselfishly to others in true need who can better use you than you can, you may find that you can also ameliorate your pain.

Day 26
Forgiveness

Bless... Your Ex?

We've saved the question of forgiving that person who you may feel has grievously wronged you for near the end of your healing. We've done so because we know how difficult this process might be.

Oh, you may already say that you have no bad feelings about your ex. But does your anger and pain still show through to those who know you best? Or are you one of those people who loathe the idea of blessing, much less forgiving or even having a single decent thought about the other party in a past romance that turned sour?

Forget the fact that you were originally responsible for involving yourself with this person. Ignore the fact that you must have seen something good in them then, good enough to risk putting your heart on the line. Just remember that if you don't let *all* of your feelings for this person go completely, even your feelings of malice will keep you mired in the past.

If you should find yourself not just telling but *selling* anyone on just how rotten your former lover really was, you not only run the risk of inviting that someone to think less of your integrity, you run the danger of turning them off. If a new friend or worse, someday, a new lover should hear this kind of bitterness from you, they will quite naturally worry when their turn as targets in your barrel might be coming.

That's the problem with bitterness. It's like a cup with an uneven lip. Whenever you drink from it, you don't know when your malice will spill in your lap. Worse yet, if you entertain ill feelings about your past, they will almost always show up when others enter your life, even if you pretend that those feelings are not part of your scene any more.

You loved your ex at one time. All of your dreams and plans may have been built around him or her. So when your dreams were wrested away from you, you felt you were stranded. You certainly never wanted to feel so alone. As a result, it may have seemed a lot easier to blame someone else for your anguish than to take responsibility for yourself, and to evolve.

Yes, someone you loved may have betrayed your trust. As a result, you may now say that you hate that person, or at least feel profoundly disappointed by their behavior. But if you truly disdain what they've done to you, why do you still want to be controlled by them?

You will, for just so long as you give such embittered feelings dominion over your future hopes.

That's why you need to bless your ex. You also need to do this *not* with your teeth gritted, or while pasting on a strained smile to hold back your rage. You really need to whole-heartedly bless this person in order to let them go. You need to wish them the very best for their life. You even need to be genuinely gratified if they've found better and deeper contentment with another. You need to do this because even if they didn't do their best loving you, perhaps their new situation will finally bring out the best they can offer.

By letting this person go, you liberate yourself to love and be loved in a truly free manner. Of course, this isn't the easiest thing to accomplish. For many it's far easier just to hang onto anger. That way, they don't have to work anything out. They can just wallow in bitter self-righteousness.

The prescription for such self-corrosion is sweetness itself. But in fact, it can be quite hard to swallow.

Start by telling the story of you and your ex, and of all of the disappointments this person inflicted on you. Describe how you were let down, how you were put down. Now take the "you" out of the story. And as you do, remove all of your rancor, all of your resentment, all of your desire for love or revenge. Take them out, if just for a painful moment, and see what's left. You will find revealed just another human being struggling to find their own way to happiness.

Then describe all of the lessons this person taught you.

When you've done this, reflect on the importance of these lessons to the rest of your life. Then, in your mind and heart only (*don't* call them or write to them), thank this person for all of that they helped you to learn. The gentle lessons were blessings; the hard ones will help you to avoid such pain for the rest of your life. Both kinds are treasures, for which you can thank your teachers, and wish them well. And then… bid them goodbye.

This is the one step that will most powerfully detoxify your feelings. If you can take this step, you'll see that after even the worst endings, even after those moments when there's only rage, and grief, and disappointment, in time you'll be able to appreciate memories of what was fun, exciting and meaningful about your times together. You will thereby nurture the everloving optimism that shyly awaits its release in each of our hearts. And all from blessing your ex and all of his or her happiest dreams.

Now that you've blessed them, naturally you'll hope for the best for them. But you also release them from all responsibility for your own challenges. They are on their own now to learn and to do as they must. If you still must negotiate any financial or custodial issues with them, you can now do so dispassionately. You can confidently and adamantly assert your own best interests, just as you would with anyone else with whom you may have a dispute.

Resolving disputes should never soil your regard for yourself and the worth of your love. You have a great richness within you to share with others, and many new dreams you now need to make happen. Remember that your ability to give and receive love is the source of your new power. Just walk into a room, smile from your heart while you hold your head high. Then watch what happens…

 . . . Make Love To Strangers

Robert Mungerson, the late, great Chicago therapist, often drove home the following point: "It's easiest to share intimacy with perfect strangers. It's a little harder to be honestly intimate with acquaintances, where the risks of our self-disclosures may carry a penalty. And a lot harder to do with friends, because the price of our truths may be to risk a relationship we value. To be truly intimate with a lover carries the greatest risk of all..."

That's the price we pay for relationships. And what too often accounts for their endings. Yet intimacy and a loving, unconditioned acceptance of another deeply valued person, remains a condition to which most healthy people aspire.

How do we do that? How do we dare?

Is there any way to go back to school on loving, to learn how to better deal with the pain that rejection or loss can bring?

In a word: Yes.

Love School.

We urge you to try the following exercise at your earliest opportunity. It's an eye opener that may even cause you to believe you have latent telepathic abilities. Incidentally, we have no idea whether or not you may or may not have such a skill. What this exercise can produce if you do it properly is simply an intensive experience of empathy with another human being, on a totally unconditioned basis.

How do you do this? Easy: start making love to strangers. There's no need to worry about sexually transmitted diseases, either. We're not urging you to have sex with anyone. You don't even have to talk to anyone. You're just going to make love with your eyes, and your heart, secretly. Only you will know that you're making love to someone.

All we'd like you to do is to find a spot in a heavily trafficked public place where you can sit quietly, without being noticed. But your seat should make it easy for you to observe other passers-by for several seconds to minutes at a time.

Find someone in the crowd on whom to focus your attention. Watch their movements while you do something that may make you feel odd: love the person you're watching. If it makes it easier for you to do what you need to, say over and over again to yourself: "I love you." If you're successful, you may experience a physical feeling of expansiveness in your chest, a sense of a door within opening as you secretly expose yourself to this act of loving a stranger, even if they never even notice your existence.

If you correctly do this exercise as we've described it, you should immediately be rewarded by a strange sense of familiarity. You will somehow sense the feelings that the person you have chosen to love is experiencing at that moment, whether consciously or otherwise. Be prepared: more people than you expect are likely to convey feelings of sadness, isolation or loneliness. Given your own recent losses, this might even offer you some comfort, to know that many people share your own current state.

Practice this exercise as often as you can, until you can quickly and easily love a stranger at a moment's glance. Then try watching a friend when they aren't paying you any attention. How much do you dare love them? What fears are holding you back? Or if you succeed, what does this active loving teach you about your friend that you didn't know before?

And think of how much fun it will be someday for you to perfect your ability to love in this exciting new way, with someone that you really want to share all of your heart.

Day 27 Idealism

Opening Your Heart Surgery

One of the reasons you still feel wounded may be emotional diabetes. Has your system overdosed on sweet sentimentality? To see if it's so, test yourself: do you feel that you must have things that no longer exist?

It's too cute a trick to blame the absence of things from your past for the presence of your problems. Too cute because no one can argue with you. You're right. The past happened. Bad stuff happened. So it sounds almost reasonable for you to shrink from taking new chances or to stop learning new things. "Once burned, twice careful." Play the game hard enough and no one will argue with your embittered spirit. With one exception. He's called father.

Father Time, of course.

Imagine that you've been blessed with total amnesia. Without your memories, you'd now feel no pain. Granted, you'd also be as ignorant as a pig. But that may now seem to be a small price to pay.

But you don't have to pay that price. Time takes care of that for us. Memory is a fragile blessing at best. Time will erase your most hurtful memories first, and then help you to set the stage for new options. But time also ages us. Time says, "Don't stay paralyzed forever or new opportunities will die." That's a frightening thought. It often exposes as hollow those no longer meaningful relationships that unhappy people use to avoid facing the truth that their love really has died.

If you really want to exchange romantic love with someone again someday, if you really want to live a life enlightened by love, offer them love in a truly open hearted fashion. If you really want the love of another to be real in this world, *don't need them*. That's the surest way to stop acting like the frightened animals we too often are. Fear's how we chase away our best prospects, just when we want to reach out to them most.

Romance's battlegrounds are littered with carnage. Dead and dying marriages fill up the field. Broken hearts lie shattered wherever you turn. So it's easy to see why you might shrink from any real commitment to anyone else. It's hard not to be moved by all the war stories. Yes, it calls for courage today to take a shot at true happiness. We all know how many people ended up going through hell. Yet even if you have a long history of relationship disappointments, how sad to be stuck in those old war stories and so lose chances to explore better ways.

Usually the villains of your own romantic war stories will by now be gone from your life. Often the villains are people that you may have loved at one time but finally realized that you didn't like very much. So why on earth would you let these fabled figures from your past run your life now? If you do, then they will win your future, too. And you lose.

An urban legend has attained common currency among today's veteran victims of the Romantic Wars. Their shared fantasy is not of a dream-relationship with Dick and Jane furnishings: a home, a spouse, a baby and a dog. That pretty dream is part of the past. Today's favored legend has tragic overtones. It's the sour belief that no loving relationship can reliably reward its participants for any extended period of time. "He'll never have enough money." "She will never be confident enough." And once he does have enough money or once she finds her center, new excuses arise.

For life to be meaningful, you have to commit to something larger than safety. It's not necessary for you to commit yourself to someone else. But you must commit to *something*. There is absolutely no avoiding commitment if happiness is to be won. If you can commit to a life of sharing your love, it will happen. If you commit to poisoning your heart with doubt and mistrust, that's still a commitment. But unfortunately, in this case life will reward you by withholding any meaningful or joyous relationships in your life.

The moment you stop blaming others, the moment you open your heart to loving; that's the moment in which your life will change for the better. That's also the moment when you will discover that you don't need to limit yourself to halfway relationships that will only result in our feeling more empty, tepid, and bitter than ever.

Your intimacies will almost certainly falter if you expect a new lover to heal your old love wounds, or worse, to act as a stand-in for the failings of others. These innocents, those who want to give love to you and who want to receive your love in exchange, can be cast as unwitting characters in your saddest old plays. So the inevitable happens. These new people in your life become the victims of your projected and unresolved anger at a figure from your past. So your past may become a vehicle to bring out the worst in good people in your present or future.

Psychoanalyst Carl Jung said "An ideal relationship is when two parties swim together in the same ocean but then return to their respective shores." The more secure you are in the truth of yourself, the less threatened you'll be by embracing another in a truthful and loving intimate relationship. When you surrender your need to worry about how a loved one feels about you, you then earn the freedom to give love to another, and be loved in return. Now doesn't that sound like a far better feeling than enforcing a connection through manipulations of fear and anxiety?

Think about your shore. Is it a warm, sunny place that someone you'd find attractive would want to spend time in? Or has it become a dark swamp that you seduce others to swim in just so you can keep your waters as bitter as habit inclines you? What simple attitude shifts can you engineer that will clean up your shore and transform it into a pleasant place full of love and support? You can do this in any way you choose.

You can do all of this easily once you understand that you're meant to be joyous and fulfilled. Again, this understanding represents a commitment, a commitment to the knowledge that it's your natural birthright to simply be happy. Once you understand and believe this, you will have already cleaned up your shore.

For some of our readers, their full recovery will prove to be just this easy. For them, it can be done by making a deeply personal choice. But others among you may still need more support, more interventions by friends, more books, more time, perhaps even counseling. But *whatever* it takes to truly reopen your heart to love and be loved, please do it as soon as you can.

 **. . . Change The Scale**

One of the standard tactics for "getting over your ex" is to work on changing the scale of your ex's importance to you. After all, that person who was once the most important thing in your life will soon enough be nothing but a memory, and perhaps not a significant one at that.

But *knowing* that is not the same as *feeling* it, yet. How can you reduce their importance to you, right now? One way to start the process of their shrinkage is to rehearse for the worst; once you're ready for that, you can begin to see that right now things aren't so bad after all. Another way to put things in perspective is to talk about how you feel about things more carefully, without adding any false drama that may only make you feel worse. And a final way to put your past in the past is to have a ritual burning, to exorcise your demons...

Imagine The Worst

If you still see your former lover as an attractive but lost cause, imagine the worst. For example, imagine that you've been invited to a "I have to attend" event where everyone you know and care about will be present. Your ex will be there too, with another person who seems to be your successor. How will you cope with your feelings of embarrassment and jealousy?

Now imagine the situation in detail. Imagine your responses to the conversation you have when your ex introduces you to your replacement. See yourself as acting in a mature and dignified way. Invent some truly witty dialogue to use in response to every remark anyone present may make. Imagine how many ways you can "win" this situation. Enjoy seeing yourself as a noble and tragic figure seen from all angles. Imagine how much your friends and family who are present will admire how masterfully you've managed to handle yourself.

Work your way through constructing this fantasy in such excruciating detail you become utterly bored with imagining the whole thing. How long does it take before you realize that: (1) "this is stupid! If this were to happen, I'm totally prepared for it, and I don't really need to fear any pain." And (2) "this is stupid because I'm bored with it because it doesn't matter all that much after all."

Incidentally, if something like this really does happen to you, focus on just acting as politely and correctly as you possibly can to make the importance of the encounter dwindle into less than life-changing significance.

Talk A Good Game

One very experienced and right-thinking traveler says that if he can walk out of an airplane then he considers it a very good flight. His attitude shows that the way we talk about the things that happen to us determines how we feel about them. "Air turbulence?

No problem; we landed safely, after all." Save the "it's been a bad day" statements for days when you wake up in a hospital bed…

In short, choose your language more carefully. Someone really is listening: it's you. If you tell yourself that losing your ex is the worst thing that ever happened to you, at that moment it will seem to be so. But if you can simply say that your breakup has been stressful but that you're confident you'll get over it soon, you'll make your job of recovery a lot easier. As a matter of fact, this kind of plain speech is both more modest and probably accurate than trying to make yourself sound like a martyr to yourself or anyone else.

Ritual Cleansing

One final way to put things in perspective: burn up your memories. Save one photo and one love note, and do one of three things with all of the rest of the mementos from your former relationship:

1.   Send them back to the other party, if you are on civil terms and wish to keep it that way. But don't use this act as a reason to see the other party again. The Post Office can do this job for you nicely.

2.   Make up a ritual for yourself. Burn these "unkeepsakes" in a fire, and cast their ashes into the waters of the largest nearby lake, ocean or river. As you do so, watch these tokens of your past go away from your present and future.

3.   Throw all of this junk in the trash, without giving it a second thought. Hey! There you go! All right for you!

Day 28 Gratitude

Thanksgiving Day

How outrageous a thought! Your heart was broken and some authors who are strangers to you suggest that you give thanks? Here you are still completing the healing of one of the great hurts of your life. Doesn't it seem like the last thing you need is some sermonizing cheerleader telling you to be thankful?

Breakups usually deliver either pain or relief ("Phew! I'm glad that's finally over"). But for most people, even the person who plays "the dumper," a void has opened. And when a void has displaced love and joy, sour feelings are too often used to fill in the cracks. When your old familiar world has fallen apart in this way, it's expected that you'll burrow into mourning and complain that nothing is going your way. What's to be thankful for now! Who cares!

Yet, there's a theory that a person's civility, their mastery of maturity and the manners that go with it, may be most readily gauged by their ability to simply say thank-you.

In contrast to this, whatever we neglect, slight, and fail to appreciate will usually be taken away from us. That means that a breakup often delivers both parties good reason to realign their values by learning, perhaps more honestly than ever before, what they treasure, and what they do not.

Suppose you lost not just your central relationship, but your job and your home, along with your car and all income. That would certainly be a desperate situation. Now how could you still find joy? Can you think of anything left that you value?

It's certainly hard to feel joy when you're in the middle of a panicky state. But to take this example, you may still have your good health and the love of your family. Perhaps you have the affection of a faithful pet. You probably still can take a walk by the shore or a hike in the mountains. You can be thankful for the fresh air, for the new day and a new chance, and the freedom to create a new and better adventure in your life.

This exercise will call forth different losses for everyone, but the basic process is always the same. By giving up the first things you think you have, or had, you should be able to see what remains and give intense thanks for it. Even if it's just for the privilege of breathing the air, or trading a smile.

When you see the immensity in the gift of even the smallest of things, the results become cumulative. All of your life begins to rebuild itself, around a deeper awareness of values.

So, is this really such an outrageous time for you to feel gratitude? Or is this a perfectly wonderful moment for you to discover gratitude for the gift of existence? Maybe your only sensible course is to outgrow your old self and become aware of the simple gifts that you've too long taken for granted.

You were born giving and receiving love. You're still a fully equipped lover. You are complete and able to love in every way that's humanly possible. But if you close yourself off to this ground of your existence, how are happier aspects ever going to find their way into your life? Even more importantly, how are you going to know completely that you *are* alive?

Despite this, many love-beaten people clearly signal their warnings: they don't trust other people. And they feel very destructive. In truth, everyone wants to experience love in some way. Too many people feel lost and worthless. It's their sense of unworthiness that has injured and frightened them into hiding behind their hostility. Too many are delivered into a bitter old age, with none of the things that really matter, like sharing of their love with children, animals, or any significant other. All because they lacked the humility, the maturity, the strength that's needed to lift their heads upward to say "thank-you."

So if that sounds something like you, stop running from the truth. It's simple and it says, "love life."

Try this simple exercise: in the next three minutes look for three significant things you can be deeply grateful for. Do you have the courage to find these things and give real thanks? These simple things, the sky, the air, a smile, are the solid foundations for your future happiness

 . . . Open Your Escape Hatch

You know what conventional wisdom has to say about the pain of your loss, that "you can run, but you

can't hide" from it. But that's only partially true. There are three things you can do to put some distance between yourself and your painful loss:

1. Go someplace new that will open your eyes.

2. Look for beauty in new places and new ways.

3. Meet new people; they can help you to heal.

Here's some ideas about why and how to do each of these things.

New Views

Educators believe that we learn more through our eyes than any of our other senses. So now is the time to learn a new way to look at the world, freshly and on your own. As soon as you can, start taking small trips to places that offer a fresh perspective. Even if your wallet won't permit you to take that cruise of a lifetime just yet, hop on the bus and ride it all the way out to the end of the line.

If no friends are available to join you, there's no shame at all in going by yourself to the museum or a concert, little theater performances, or even on a weekend-long getaway. Is it time for a new hobby? One recent Gallup survey revealed that people derive more pleasure from learning than from sex or winning the lottery. And at the least, learning something interesting can divert your attention away from your pain. Sign up for a class at the local college or university, or just check out a good book at the local library.

Beauty Alert

In your travels to new places, or even to old

ones, pay attention: look and listen for beautiful things. Our recognition of beauty is sometimes held to be one of the ways that God shows us he or she exists. Even if beauty is no more profound than a happy accident, it still provides us with a source of inspiration that's available everywhere (if you look for it), at no charge whatsoever.

To help keep yourself alert in your search for beauty, carry a camera or a pair of binoculars. Taking a photo of something that you find attractive can help train your eye to always scan your surroundings, looking for something that can make you feel joyful.

Sometimes, we ignore beauty just because we fail to pay attention to it. Next time you go out, listen for the sound of a song bird while you look at the clouds pass through the sky.

Open To Strangers

You won't really be ready to take on a new lover until you've gotten over the last one. But just because you're "out of the market" doesn't mean that meeting new people is out of the question. In fact, making new acquaintances and friends can help you restore your sense of self-esteem, and provide you with a more objective sounding board for your problems than can those who already have an investment in your relationship with your ex.

How do you go about meeting new people? We have two suggestions: stay out of bars, and borrow a dog. Why the dog? Because research has shown that dog's are one of the best ice breakers with strangers that have ever been invented. Researchers at The University of Warwick discovered that any kind of a dog makes it easier for two strangers to interact with each other. It didn't matter whether either the dog walker or dog looked scruffy or svelte, the pooch still lubricated the chances for a social connection. As the study's author Dr. June McNicholas said, "This may help us understand why pet owners are frequently reported to be healthier than non-owners. It may be that increased casual social contact can increase feelings of well-being, provide companionship and a sense of social integration."

Whether you borrow or buy a dog for this purpose or not, make it a point to chat with at least one stranger or new acquaintance every day. Within a month, two or three can wind up as friends, and perhaps key assets for the rest of your life.

$\mathcal{D}ay$ 29 $\mathcal{P}reparation$

A World of New Encounters

The initial goal of this book was to give you the tools you needed to ward off stress and depression. Our final goal is to help you find the strength needed to heal your emotional wounds. Once again, let us reiterate that you can't promote healing by jumping into a replacement relationship. And that vowing to be a secular monastic in hopes of acquiring some kind of contemplative wisdom will be equally unwise for most of our readers.

All we urge you to do is raise your awareness in order to make better choices, whatever or whenever those choices may be. For example, some of you may have strong enough stomachs to try dating almost immediately. As long as your purpose is strictly self-educational, this might be an instructive experience. After being in an intimate relationship for a while, people often forget their dating skills. But if your initial dating experiments go sour, then you may become soured on the prospects and process. It's like seeing a bad movie. Once you do, you don't want to go see another one for a while.

If you do rush into a new relationship even though you know it's not perfect, you may believe it will give you a way to create distance between you and your ex. Some people even take refuge in such a modest affair because they know it will protect them from the risks of a deeper and more demanding kind of sharing. Our judgment aside, all we will say to such people is: pay attention. You're still healing. The choices you make now can help or set back all of your progress.

By elevating your awareness you should attain a broad new perspective. The greater range of your view will help you to more clearly see your new opportunities. Some may turn up quickly. The best will take a while to perceive. We're not saying that you should hold back from dating or socializing. You're certainly not a child and you don't deserve to be punished. We just urge you to maintain your standards whenever you socialize.

You are finally learning to define yourself as just who you are, not as a mate who is tied to another. When you can take joy in that fact, your future opportunities will of course become greater. As you heal and begin to look around once again, here's a checklist to help afford you some guidance. Give all of these ideas time to take hold.

1. How do you feel? People can read a lack of self-confidence in your eyes. Here's a cruel fact: it's a turnoff. Don't amble among strangers until you're easily able to step out with a smile and keep your head held high.

If you project a sense of vulnerability, you may attract a rescuer. That someone may give you emotional support in exchange for your love. But beware, basing your dealings on this kind of dependency may stunt your emotional evolution.

2. How do you look? Do you look your best? Have you let yourself go? Do you need to get back in shape or restyle your hair?

If you project a sloppy and uncaring image, you'll most likely attract the lowest common-denominators into your life.

3. Where do you look? How do you meet people? What kinds of places make you feel comfortable about talking with strangers? Do you have a list of places you can go with friends.? Do you use a dating service?

4. How are your social skills? Were you once a good flirt? Are you still? Can you laugh easily and make other people laugh with you? Do you see yourself as someone you'd want to spend time with? Or are you showing even the least little bit of desperation?

5. Practice making new friends and acquaintances every day of the week. The best loves are often born of genuine friendships.

6. When you want to develop more depth and meaning to any relationship, seek to meet your own emotional needs first, rather than trying to satisfy the expectations that the other person may have.

7. Don't be a "pleasure pig." Stay away from high-speed fantasy flings. Don't simply seek the visceral thrill of making a conquest. If you keep falling and flailing your way into and out of what you may somehow call love, you'll end up running in circles rather than growing. Recognize where your true satis-

faction comes from and work patiently towards that end.

8. Before you even consider falling in love with anyone again, get a sense of where the other person may take you. Seek out their hearts and the beauty within them before you seek to do anything else.

9. Look for love in a lot of new places and ways. Perhaps the reason you've got a track record for hurting is that you've made the same mistakes with each new relationship. And just because someone responds to your overtures doesn't mean they will be suitable for you. Romance may be magic but its spells are by no means easy to master.

10. Don't make any new lover pay for your old traumas. Don't look for new love to cure your old ills. That's your job, not theirs.

11. Learn how to cut your losses more quickly. Keep your emotional bags packed and parked by the door, until you're absolutely sure this one's for you. If you don't have a good feeling about someone, move on quickly but as graciously as possible. Otherwise you'll pay the price of dealing with more pain.

12. Don't show off the scars from your past relationships. New prospects may only conclude you're a professional victim and head for the hills.

13. Take stock of who you are privately, when you're relaxed, with your guard down. That's the real you, the person you should project when you're ready to openly pursue a compatible mate.

14. Give people a chance, but don't ignore your

instincts. Be a good interior detective, especially about your own needs. Acknowledge it early if you're likely to face irreconcilable differences down the road. Even if love seems strong at the outset, unresolved issues can eventually undermine that foundation.

Then there are questions of beauty and character. Of course, beauty is only skin-deep, but its charms can cut to the bone. Yet as even the mirror told Snow White's stepmother, beauty can become ugly if it masks a cold heart. Our own culture usually overvalues our visual appetites, undercutting our perceptions of the beauty of good character. In the real world of loving relationships, physical beauty's second place finishers are often the most attractive inside. And remember: mere beauty invariably wilts over time, while fine character can bloom into wisdom.

Are you willing to learn to relax and accept all of the games people play in the course of their socializing? Are you also willing to risk sharing your truth, so you might discover new opportunities for growth?

Go ahead. Mix with the world. Even if you're far from ready to fall back in love, just find new interactions that you genuinely enjoy.

Take the small, safe steps of a child if you must, in order to get yourself back out there again. Meet new people by mixing in familiar groups and in casual circumstances at first. The small positive social steps you take can pay off in friendships almost immediately. You may someday choose to take romantic chances again, but only after getting your feet back on the ground. That's when you'll be able to make wiser choices.

The form your future happiness takes is completely up to you. You are the artist that will color the rest of your life. Give yourself the freedom you need to find your own beauty.

 . . . Say "Boo" To Fear

Think of your mind as a racing car. It goes so fast it's sometimes dangerous to its driver. You are capable of proceeding from point A to point C with such blinding speed that you never even notice that you passed through point B on your way to C.

How can that hurt you? Simple: it permits you to deny the truth of your experiences, in perfect sincerity. Perhaps the best example of such behavior is illustrated when you express feelings ranging from irritation to rage. How did you get there? Most times, you have instantly passed from experiencing the cause of your anger, to the experience of your feelings of wrath. You probably aren't even aware that you may have passed through two other feelings on your way to anger:

1. Awareness of your vulnerability, the potential that the new development which will provoke you threatens to undermine your sense of self-worth, and…

2. …fear. Fear which you experience as anything from uneasiness to terror…

Essentially, fear is often (always?) what really makes us "lose our temper." What we really have lost, at least for the moment, is our faith in the future. How does that work? Well, let's examine your own circumstances. Do you feel any anger toward your former lover? Whether you were the one who did the dumping or were the one who was abandoned by another, its usually the rule that anger served as fuel for a lot of the behavior that led up to, and that now follows, your separation from your ex.

What kind of fears do many people feel that fuels their anger when relationships end? Let's look at some examples of such fears. We'd suggest that you be honest with yourself as we name these fears, and answer the question: how many of these fears do you recognize in your own mind?

• "I'm going to look like an unattractive fool to others and myself."

• "The pain that I feel now is crushing me. It feels like it's going to handicap my emotional development for the rest of my life."

• "How could I have been so stupid? I can't trust myself to decide who I can trust anymore."

• "I'm financially ruined. I will never be able to recover from the material losses that this breakup will cause."

Or if you really want to play the fear game hardball style, your messages may sound like this:

• "No-one will ever love me again. I've wasted the best years of my life."

• "I'm going to find myself out on the street/all alone in the world/pushing around a shopping cart that holds all that I own…"

We don't deny that such outcomes are real possibilities which might result from a breakup. However, you will notice that all of these fears deal with possible *future* events that HAVEN'T HAPPENED YET. And they don't *HAVE* to happen, ever, either.

In short, your fears probably aren't real, yet. They are things that may or may not happen, in part based on what you do to avoid their occurrence. No, you cannot control the outcome. But by doing your best to avoid what you fear, you may never have to face the actual prospect that motivated your action.

So what does that say about anger? Basically, it says that your rages are usually wasted, because they express your fear of something that isn't quite real, at least yet. And that you may be able to avoid if you keep your head clearer, and face your vulnerability and your fears directly before you decide to blow a fuse.

It's an approach that might wind up saving you a considerable amount of money in divorce attorney's fees. Or that at the least, can help you to save face for your next big romance.

Day 30 Renewal

Graduation

What a magnificent opportunity you now have! What a wonderful adventure awaits you. And here you are, reborn in the light shed by all of your new insights about what will make life so much more fulfilling, sustaining and strength-giving. Even loving, if there's a next time around. What an exciting prospect, just to be alive!

Can't you feel it?

No? Oh, well, so you're not quite there yet. You *were* there, or so you thought, when you were in L-O-V-E. Love, sweet love, that magic non-medical cure-all, that undying hunger that demands to be fed. And of course, let's not forget the mind-altering flow of endorphins. Not even chocolate can match it, quite. Oh, yes, that was nice! Wouldn't you love to have that feeling again, being the addictive creature you are?

Now get rational, just for a moment, and think about what endorphins actually do. They're your brain's primitive equivalent of morphine, a self-manu-factured euphoria drug. And it does what other drugs like it can do: it masks pain. Yet love shouldn't be used as a means to mask pain. If it is, it's eventually going to lose its pain-relieving side effect. That's when you wind up in worse shape than before you first discovered this addictive drug.

That's when you find yourself not in L-O-V-E but in *P-A-I-N.*

Love conquers fools as well as the wise. Too many people get trapped swinging wildly between a blissful obliviousness and disappointed frustration. There's no happy landings for these desperate souls. Their bliss, while it lasts, certainly feels like perfect love. If you're in it, you may insist, glassy-eyed (feeling no pain, of course), that it's true love, uncut. Later, when your fires of bliss have burned into cinders, love is all that you asked for, yet nothing was there. Who can explain why it died? It can't have, you say, because *"love conquers all."*

Love actually may. But first you must recognize it in all of its many expressions and disguises, especially when it passes through your own heart.

It is now time to take these insights and broaden your understanding of what love really is. And in doing so, you'll never have to look for love again. Because it will find you every day, in everything from the laughter of a child to the caress of the wind.

This book is about much more than healing; it's about learning how not to get so deeply wounded by losses, and about ways to take your mind and your body to a far stronger level than you've ever enjoyed before. To give you strength not for winning contests or games, but for just loving, free of fear, free of guilt, free of shame.

💡TIP . . . The Heart's Garden

Remember when you fell in love with your ex? Your heart was ready for a romantic involvement. The core of your being was open to romance. As long as the romance lasted, you were nourished by your love. When your love died, gradually or suddenly, you found yourself cultivating a relationship that no longer bore fruit. Your feelings of love could no longer nourish your emotional needs.

It takes time to prepare your heart's garden for a new planting, and even longer for such an involvement to take root. Worse, if you involve yourself in a romance while pretending to be true to another, long-standing love, the odds of your second, secret relationship becoming successful for life will be reduced by your failure to be truthful to the first.

Some people decide to completely give up on cultivating romance after one or more too-painful failures. We have no quarrels with this choice. Women may say that they're tired of washing other people's underwear; men may say they're tired of being taken to the cleaners. Say whatever you like; so long as you remain open to the healing power of love in at least some of its myriad forms, romance can be considered to be a disposable option in your prescription for happiness.

But most people do choose to cultivate new romantic relationships. Hope springs perennial: according to the Census Bureau, 64% of all divorced women eventually remarry. The figure is close to the same for men. And many of those who divorce will ultimately remarry a former spouse. Whoever divorcees may choose to remarry, unfortunately, one in four will get divorced once again.

As they say, timing is everything. When should you start to rebuild your garden?

For most people, thirty days is just too short a time to think about dating again. We assume that by now you're through with even trying to see or speak to your ex. Hopefully, you're even over the crying jags and beating up pillows to vent your rage. But you won't be ready to really open yourself to another love until you finally can forgive or forget your grievances with your ex.

In fact, to really relate to a prospective new mate in a positive, wholesome, productive manner, you'll need to feel good about your life once again. You can't behave like a victim who's been poisoned by biting one of love's unripe fruit. Once you get *really* well, *then* you can begin to seriously date. Until then, you're just shopping. Because the best prospects will be sensitive enough to sense your negative attitude, you'll probably wind up scaring the good ones away. And that may only amplify the pain that you feel.

Dating can be an adventure, or a drag. If you're planning on dating to keep your mother off of your back, or to keep up with the folks at the office, forget it. Tell the friends who want to fix you up to wait. Stand on the sidelines until your stomach is ready for the roller coaster ride. Be sure your sense of humor is in top working condition; you're going to need it when you do date again.

How do you know when you're really ready?

Start by asking yourself if you can now accept rejection as a tasteless act rather than as a knife in the heart. Ask yourself if you're now smart enough not to involve yourself with someone who's already committed to somebody else. Can you handle talking with a new love interest about what went wrong with your last relationship? Someone who really cares about you may be curious. Can you accept that interest and respond maturely? Can you manage to deal with differences with someone new in a more positive and productive manner than you did with your ex? Can you learn from your errors in your last relationship, and do better the next time?

Make a list of how you will do that. Write it down. Save it in a place where you can find it, and read it again when you need it.

Can you tell someone else that you don't really wish to involve yourself with them in a kind and positive, yet completely honest manner? Reject them without harm? Are you ready to deal with the fearful sense that someone else is so attractive, so compellingly appealing, that they may actually have some kind of power to influence your feelings? How afraid are you, of love itself? Can you really afford to open your heart to a new romantic seed? Are you really ready to accept love from another? Or do you still have a need to punish someone for having the nerve to care about you?

Confused? Take comfort in knowing that happiness can still be yours. If some pain still lingers, draw solace from knowing you are far from alone. "Misery loves company?" No: "time heals all wounds."

To deal with whatever pain still ails you, keep using our exercises and tips. If you haven't had time to follow through on all of them, or the patience, go back now that you feel a bit calmer, and try them again. Your persistant efforts will change your life for the better.

Pain aside, even if your loss at first seemed like the very worst experience you have ever, *ever*, lived through, you've probably begun to understand it. So understand this, more deeply: loss and recovery are part of a natural process. It's actually a necessary part of the entire cycle of destruction and creative rebirth that generates our wholeness. So don't be surprised if, someday, you find yourself looking back on this time of your recovery as being far richer in significance, and ultimately more rewarding, than the experiences you recall from your romantic relationship.

Love, loss, injury and recovery are some of the most powerful teaching tools given to us by life's designer. Embrace their cycle: renew your own meanings. Now's the time to relieve your heart of the weight of your loss so you may once again rise to the healing powers of love. It surrounds you always.